DON'T QUIT...

Get Back In The Fight!

DR. EDISON NOTTAGE

Don't Quit...Get Back In The Fight!
REVISED EDITION
ISBN – 978-0-9976007-0-4
Copyright 2011 by Edison E. Nottage

Published By:
Edison Nottage Ministries, International
www.believersfaith.com
Printed in the United States of America

Unless otherwise indicated, all Scripture quotations are taken from the King James Study Bible ©1988 by Liberty University: Thomas Nelson Publishers, Nashville and The Amplified Bible ©1987 by the Zondervan Corporation and the Lockman Foundation, Grand Rapids, Michigan.

DEDICATION

This book is dedicated to all those to whom life has dealt some hard blows. When confronted with your dilemma, you might have been knocked down but you were not knocked out. Somehow, you received the faith and courage to rise again and "*get back in the fight.*"

To my best friend, ministry tag-team partner and wife, Prophet Dr. Mattie Nottage, thank you for your love and dedication to me, our family and ministry. Your selfless acts of kindness, sacrifice, profound vision and unwavering strength remind me of what the kingdom is all about. I love and appreciate you!

To all of my children, thank you for your motivation, love and continued support. *I love you all!* And finally to my mother-in-law who continues to demonstrate a great life of faith and commitment to God, even in the midst of her hard times. *God bless you!*

ACKNOWLEDGEMENT

"....the people that know their God shall be strong and do great exploits." (Daniel 11:32)

I count it an honor and a privilege to be a vessel used by God in these last days. So without reservation God will always be first in my life and given all the glory, honor and praise. I acknowledge the Holy Spirit and His power which is at work in my life, transforming me daily, more into the image of Christ.

To my darling wife, Prophetess Mattie Nottage and our children, God bless you all!

To my spiritual sons and daughters of Believers Faith Outreach Ministries, Nassau, Bahamas and Believers Faith Breakthrough Ministries, South Florida, thank you. Your prayers and support have been a source of encouragement and strength to me.

FOREWORD:
THE MAN, THE MENTOR, THE MINISTRY

It gives me great pleasure to foreword this life-changing book by my esteemed husband, Dr. Edison Nottage. He is a mighty, yet humble man of God. I have seen God use him in tremendous ways over the years to foster phenomenal change in the lives of scores of people, including mine. His powerful and prophetic preaching, candid and practical teachings, coupled with a keen sense of discernment has helped to deliver and set many captives free.

I was privileged to read this book firsthand and I believe that everyone who reads it will be infused with a new mindset that you will not quit.

If you cannot seem to put all of your questions, disappointments and frustrations into words, then this book is designed to help you articulate what you may be or have been going through. As you read this book, allow the Holy Spirit of God to speak to you. Through these pages, you will find help and encouragement. You will be empowered to succeed at the goals that God has set for you and the personal ones you have set for yourself.

Furthermore, you will uncover practical strategies that will help you defeat your giants. The shackles will be released from your hands and you will be able to swing back into your life assignment.

Finally, I believe that this book will become a source of spiritual strength; for every mother who felt like giving up; for every father whose back was against the wall; every woman or man who has even been hurt; every teacher who felt they were wasting their time; every preacher who felt like walking away; every politician who thinks they have failed; every doctor who does not know where to turn; every lawyer that has lost a case;

every young person who has been afraid to dream and finally ...
"you." You, who have every reason to throw in the towel – but
you refused to quit. This book is for you. Get back in the fight and
be blessed!   - *Dr. Mattie Nottage*

TABLE OF CONTENTS

CHAPTER ONE: DON'T QUIT ...STAY IN THE FIGHT! 1
Winners Never Quit.. 2
A Champion Within You 3
Don't Let Your Baby Die 5
Do Not Curse Your Harvest 7
Succeeding At Life's Goals.. 9

CHAPTER TWO: THE TESTING OF YOUR FAITH... 13
Tests, Trials and Tribulations... 14
Your Arduous Trial.. 15
Eduring Your Tribulations.. 17
Unwavering Faith... 19
Heirs Of An Eternal Promise 20
Conquering Your Challenges.. 20
Grace 24
Leading While Bleeding.. 25
As You Lead You May Bleed 26
Keep Your Focus.. 28
The Fate Of The Hurting And Wounded 31
Not Quitting In The War Zone 32
Worrying Profits Nothing 34
A Firm Foundation.. 35
Preparation.. 36
Elevation.. 37

CHAPTER THREE: TRUSTING GOD... 39
Dealing With Adversity.. 40
Stressed Out 42
The Day My Life Changed 43
By This Time Tomorrow 45
The Spirit Of Leprosy 46
Faith Is Now And Now Is Faith... 50

CHAPTER FOUR: WHAT GOD HAS FOR YOU... 53
I'll Never Be A Slave Again.. 54
Battlefield Of The Mind 55
My Emancipation Day... 57
Something Went Very Wrong 58
Good Things "Sometimes" Come To An End.. 60
A Set Back Or A Set Up... 61
What God Has For You-It Is For You... 62
Intensify Your Seek.. 64
"Don't Run!".. 65
Anointed To Be King 66
The Process Before The Palace 67
Desparate To Stay In The Fight.. 69

TABLE OF CONTENTS CONT'D...

CHAPTER FIVE: FAITH, POWER AND GLORY **71**

A Measure Of Faith 72

I See A Cloud 72

Mountain Moving Faith 73

Faith That Overcomes 75

Crazy Faith 76

What Would You Do For A Miracle 79

CHAPTER SIX: THE ENEMIES OF YOUR FAITH **83**

Exposing Fear 84

You Can Defeat Fear 87

Plundering The Spirit Of Pride 87

Demoliting Doubt 89

Beware Of Negative Self-Fulfilling Prophecies 91

Defeating The Enemey of Doubt 92

Spiritual Paralysis 94

Rise, Take Up Thy Bed And Walk 95

A Portion Of Faith 96

A Degree Of Faith 98

Faith That Does Not Waver 102

Stabilizing Your Faith 103

Faith and Power 105

Faith and Glory 107

CHAPTER SEVEN: THE POWER OF PERSEVERANCE **111**

Surviving Your Dry Seasons 112

Common Cents Solutions 114

Dig Your Way Out Or Give Your Way Out 119

CHAPTER EIGHT: NO IS NOT FINAL **123**

"It Aint Over!" 124

No Is Not Final In Debt 126

Supernatural Debt Cancelation 127

No Is Not Final In Death 129

No Is Not Final In Disease 130

No Is Not Final When Facing Danger And Destruction 131

CHAPTER NINE: DON'T QUIT...TRY AGAIN! **133**

No Retreat, No Surrender 134

Perseverance Pays 136

Tenacity Keeps You On The Wall 137

The Miracle Of The Building 139

TABLE OF CONTENTS CONT'D...

CHAPTER TEN: BACK IN THE FIGHT **141**

Restoration Has Come 142

Recover All-A Time To Pursue 143

Your Wealthy Place 144

Anointed To Prosper 145

Slaying Your Giants 147

Your Reward Is In The Finish! 148

INDEX **150**

Meet Apostle Dr. Edison Nottage **151**

MNM Product Page 153

Ministry Contact Information 155

CHAPTER ONE

DON'T QUIT…STAY IN THE FIGHT?

WINNERS NEVER QUIT!

Someone once coined the phrase: *"Winners never quit and quitters never win!"* **To quit means to** abandon, relinquish, cease, surrender, retreat or to discontinue.

In other words, quitters are considered to be people who abandoned, gave up on and walked away from their mission or assignment. Quitters concede in the midst of battle accepting defeat rather than fighting to the end for a desired victory.

True winners do not ever concede, they are relentless in their fight and will not leave the battlefield until their opponent is defeated. If they are knocked down, they often find the strength to get up again and get back in the fight.

"We are troubled on every side, yet not distressed; we are perplexed, but not in despair; Persecuted, but not forsaken; cast down, but not destroyed."
(2 Corinthians 4:8-9)

God is looking for you regardless of how long you have been knocked out, he is counting on you to get back in the fight and stay the course.

A CHAMPION WITHIN YOU

October 1st, 1975 is recorded in the annals of history as the date of one of the greatest boxing matches of all times - Muhammad Ali vs. Joe Frazier III. From the commencement of the match, the two fought relentlessly for fourteen entire rounds. Each fighter was determined not to give up nor quit. The match was grueling and very intense. The fighters persevered through blood, sweat and tears, none willing to give in to the massive punches from the other.

Eventually, Frazier's coach seeing the agony of his boxer, threw in the towel at the end of the fourteenth round. He only had to endure one more round, the fifteenth, but he waved the white flag of surrender. The winner, Muhammad Ali, described the experience as, *"... as close to death as I have ever been."* They were both great fighters, but only one emerged victorious because he refused to give up, he simply refused to quit.

Boxing, unlike team sports is an individual sport where each person must be conditioned to endure hard knocks and blows from his opponent. The score in each round is based on the amount of blows you are able to land or the punch that is able to knock your opponent out.

Most boxers at some point in their career have had a broken nose or jaw, fractured ribs, lacerated eyes or concussions to the head; just to name a few. At some point during their match, they will agree that they all have been knocked down before; but the ones who excelled as winners were those who were knocked down or even knocked out but who eventually got back into the fight.

Ali was determined to finish. With swollen eyes and not much strength left in his knees, or a "rope a dope", he leaned on the ring ropes for support. He became the champion that day and never looked back.

You must have that same mentality, no matter who you are or no matter what situation you may find yourself in. You can achieve your dreams despite what circumstances you may find yourself in and regardless of what obstacles may be strewn across your path; do the "rope a dope" if you have to, but whatever you do, don't quit. *I stumbled across this little poem I thought you may enjoy it*

WHY – GET BACK IN THE FIGHT?

"Who knows what is laying dormant deep down inside of you? You may be on the verge of becoming the next champion or pioneer for a good cause and that is a good reason to get back in the fight!"

DON'T LET YOUR BABY DIE!
"Reactivating Dreams, Visions and Ideas"

Your *dreams* are your desired or anticipated outcomes for your life. Your *visions* represent the expectations you have for your life and are normally seen through the eyes of faith. Your *ideas* are a culmination of your plans which you seek to implement in order to obtain success in life.

Everyone at some point in life has had a dream. It may have been a prophetic dream while you were asleep or a dream which communicates your personal desire and aspirations in life, which are in alignment with the divine will of God.

It is no doubt that it is these deep seated dreams and visions that sometimes help to pave the spiritual pathway of your life, pointing you to your destiny. Satan already knows this and will send dream assassins in your way to interrupt or kill the spiritual goal God placed in your spirit inside of you.

Have you ever had a dream, vision or an idea that you finally gave birth to and, unexpectedly, it died? I am sure we have all had at least one of them. Something no doubt that you were looking forward to achieving or receiving over a long period of time finally came. And just when you started celebrating, it died.

That is one of the most painful experiences anyone can have. However, the question arises, "Do you leave it dead or do you rise up and fight for it to live again?" The Shunamite woman in *2 Kings 4* had everything she ever wanted in life except a child. The prophet Elisha prophesied to her that by the next season and according to the time of life God would give her a son.

By the next season, she conceived and bore a son. The boy grew but suddenly one day he had a headache and died. The Shunamite woman went back to the man of God and reminded him of the prophecy that he gave her and that death was not a part of it. He prayed for the boy until he came back to life.

You have a choice either to let your dreams die or pray it back to life. According to John 4, Jesus is the resurrection and the life even though your dreams may die, He can bring them back to life again.

"Your vision has an appointment with time!"
For the vision is yet for an appointed time, but at
the end it shall speak, and not lie: though it tarry,
wait for it; because it will surely come, it will not
tarry. (Habakkuk 2:3)

Every dream or vision has an appointed day or time to be fulfilled. Just as every seed planted in the ground goes through a process of germination, so must your dreams and visions.

DO NOT CURSE YOUR HARVEST
[24] Verily, verily, I say unto you, Except a corn of wheat fall into the ground and die, it abideth alone: but if it die, it bringeth forth much fruit. (John 12:24)

The seed must die first before it can live. However, given the right atmospheric conditions of soil, sun, water and carbon dioxide it sprouts and grows bearing fruit in the fullness of time.

Growing up on my grandfather's farm, I noticed he never gave up on a crop. In fact, he was so confident that his harvest would come that he would take handfuls of seed and throw them across the field. My job was to water them and pray for rain.

Granddaddy's job was to prophecy and go out to the field every now and then to weed away the wild bush from around his new corn stalks, keeping the fowls away. Every year the harvest came and granddaddy gave God praise for it.

"Death and life are in the power of the tongue..."
(Proverbs 18:21)
"...you shall have whatsoever you say..."
(Mark 11:23)

Never curse your seed by speaking death over it. When you curse your seed, you have cursed your harvest. No matter what your situations look like, speak the word of faith and life over it. God's word is spirit and life. You have the power to frame your world by your words.

"And you shall decree a thing and it shall be accomplished..." (Job 23:28)

No matter how long it appears to be taking for your seed to produce a fruit or harvest, it is your job to speak life over it ... and wait. Remember, in *Genesis 8:22*, the Word of God says that there is seed – time – and harvest.

SUCCEEDING AT LIFE'S GOALS

Success is not defined by materialistic gain or the money you may have or by how many people you have stepped on to get it, but rather it is defined by the magnitude of kingdom imprint and legacy you have left behind to better someone else's life.

It is the fact that you have made someone else's life, besides yours, better and not bitter. Furthermore, in my opinion, success without good health and the strength to enjoy it is not success at all.

Success or successful people are those who have made mistakes in life, but simply refused to quit. Furthermore, it is the fact that you have come to the profound understanding that success is not necessarily the key to you being happy, but better still, you having God and being happy; that's the key to success.

"Godliness with contentment is great gain."
(1 Timothy 6:6)

To succeed in life is to exceed and excel beyond every negative expectation, accomplishing your life's goals.

The opposite of success is failure. To fail is to give up or accept defeat as your final verdict when you have not fully tried. Success or failure is always based on the decisions you make. *"If you have failed to plan to succeed, you have already planned to fail."*

Whatever you do in this season, always remember and never forget that even FAILURE IS NOT FINAL!

I believe that people who go on to win gold medals are those who came to the event with a plan that they were going to succeed. The world will never forget Vanderlei Cordeiro de Lima from Brazil who ran the marathon during the Summer Olympics in Athens, Greece, 2004. He was leading the race at 35 km when out of nowhere a spectator jumped from the roadside and attacked him.

This incident caused him to go from first place to third place, winning the bronze medal. It was a horrific moment. Persons that were miles behind him overtook him. Much to everyone's surprise, he got up and started running again. He had trained for years and he had a goal in mind that he wanted to achieve.

Upon entering the stadium, beaten and bruised, everyone gave him a resounding applause and a standing ovation. He did not receive the gold medal for winning the race, but was later awarded the Pierre de Coubertin medal for sportsmanship just because he got up and finished the race.

"The race is not to the swift....but he who will endure to the end...." (Ecclesiastes 9:11)

If you are going to succeed in life you must have a goal. Your goal is the ultimate achievement intended or anticipated in fulfilling your endeavors. It is your single most intended desire that you are seeking to accomplish. *Each goal must have four basic components in order to achieve it:*

- There must be a Motive
- A Purpose
- An Aim
- An Objective

The Motive: establishes what is the driving force propelling you to accomplish your goal.

The Purpose: defines your original intent or reason why you have set your goal.

The Aim: focuses on your desired or intended result as you attempt to accomplish your goals

The Objective: outlines the plan or steps you put in place in order to achieve your goal

Once you have established a set goal in life and have sought God concerning it, you can begin to charter a course to accomplish it. *With the favor of God you can and will achieve it.*

"With men this is impossible; but with God all things are possible." (Matthew 19:26)

CHAPTER TWO

THE TESTING OF YOUR FAITH

TESTS, TRIALS & TRIBULATIONS
"Going Through Your Test!"

The test is considered to be a measurement of performance, reliability or quality. It is a procedure of critical evaluation and the means of determining the truth or strength of something or someone. A test is normally given to you as a result of some lesson that you have been presumably taught and/or that you should have learnt over a period of time or at a particular season of your life.

Furthermore, the purpose of the test is to ascertain your level of knowledge attained during the course of that lesson. Finally, it is to determine whether or not you moved on to a new level of elevation, higher place or if you must remain in the same position. As stated in, James 1:3, *"Think it not strange concerning the fiery trial which is to try you ..."*

Most people give up in the middle of their test, trial or tribulation. The experiences in your trial come as it says; to "try" you. The trial comes as a result of an accusation or allegation against you. Trials are, for the most part, unforeseen or unexpected. In most cases, whenever you go through a trial, it is because you are being accused by an adversary. As in every court, it is your role to prove to them that you are innocent or rather, not guilty.

Many people are accused and thrown into unforeseen trials with no idea as to how they got in them. However, their biggest frustration comes in when trying to get out of these trials.

"The trying of your faith worketh patience..."
(James 1:3)

YOUR ARDUOUS TRIAL

Going through the trial and not quitting is the key to your victory. The race is not always for the swiftest, but for those that are willing to endure to the end. Patience, in my opinion, is a virtue of the wise.

In other words, throughout history we will note that it was always wise men who took the time to master patience or *"the art of waiting"* who were able to accomplish great things. Faith builders and world changers, such as Abraham, Noah, Hannah and Solomon all have in some way or the other impacted the kingdom. For example, Solomon, a man of faith and wisdom built a billion-dollar temple and dedicated it back to God.

Other great men in our day and time, by the wisdom of God invented cars, planes, skyscrapers and formulas that had never been heard or dreamt of before. They tried and failed numerous times – they waited and kept trying.

The story is told of Thomas Edison who was credited with inventing the light bulb. Edison tried over one thousand times before he was finally able to perfect the modern day light bulb. Later, he was asked how he felt after failing over one thousand times, he simply replied, *"I have never failed, not one time. I have rather figured out one thousand ways that it cannot work."* Wow! That is patience! That is a mindset that says I am not giving up and I am not quitting until I see the breakthrough.

"Our greatest weakness lies in giving up. The most certain way to succeed is always to try just one more time." - Thomas Edison

As a result of his resilience and willingness to try again, hundreds of millions of people worldwide now enjoy the pleasantries and benefits that come with the power of the light bulb.

Likewise, where would we be without Benjamin Franklin's discovery of electricity? As a result of his research, we are now able to enjoy the benefits of fans, air condition units, automated teller machines (ATM's), monorails and much more. Thank God someone was patient enough to wait and had faith enough to believe that it could be done – and did it!

ENDURING YOUR TRIBULATION

Tribulation may be defined as going through hardship and distress as a result of oppression or persecutions. When you find yourself going through any degree of tribulation it probably means that you are doing something good.

Jesus said, *"11Blessed are ye, when men shall revile you, and persecute you, and shall say all manner of evil against you falsely, for my sake.*

12Rejoice, and be exceeding glad: for great is your reward in heaven: for so persecuted they the prophets which were before you..."
(Matthew 5:11-12)

In our society today, few people are able to relate to going through tribulation. If the truth be told, not many people stand firm in the midst of their adversity. In fact, it is sometimes much easier to blend in with the crowd, rather than stand out.

Those that endure persecution and tribulation for the sake of the cross or their faith in God receive blessings from the Father that are immeasurable.

> *"Enduring tribulation as a child of God produces a testimony. It is by our testimony and by the blood of Jesus Christ that we can overcome the enemy." (Revelation 12:11)*

> *"Many are the afflictions of the righteous but God delivers him out of them all ..."*
> *(Psalm 39:14)*

Many times people give up not knowing that they were so close to their miracle or divine blessing. The test, trial or tribulation comes to produce what I call "*strong faith.*" This is the type of faith that cannot be bought or taken away from you. It is faith that you have earned by the blood of Jesus Christ.

UNWAVERING FAITH

Can you imagine Abraham being almost one hundred (100) years old and still holding on to the promise that God gave him? He believed that God would give him a son, making him the Father of many Nations.

[19] And being not weak in faith, he considered not his own body now dead, when he was about an hundred years old, neither yet the deadness of Sarah's womb:

[20] He staggered not at the promise of God through unbelief; but was strong in faith, giving glory to God; [21] And being fully persuaded that, what he had promised, he was able also to perform
(Romans 4:19-21)

God will perform everything in your life just as He promised. It does not matter how long it takes, His promises are *"yes"* and *"amen."*

"For all the promises of God in him are yea, and in him Amen, unto the glory of God by us"
(2 Corinthians 1:20)

HEIRS OF AN ETERNAL PROMISE

God gave Abraham a son, Isaac and Abraham became the Father of many Nations. We are the seed of Abraham according to *Galatians 3:29*

"And if ye be Christ's, then are ye Abraham's seed, and heirs according to the promise."

Therefore we are heirs of an eternal promise and every blessing God has given to Abraham, belongs to you and me. "Don't Quit - get up and embrace your inheritance right now!

CONQUERING YOUR CHALLENGES

"My brethren, count it all joy when ye fall into divers temptations; Knowing this, that the trying of your faith worketh patience.

But let patience have her perfect work, that ye may be perfect and entire, wanting nothing."
(James 1:2-4)

The path of life is not always an easy one to walk. It can sometimes be compared to an obstacle course, strewn with challenges and hurdles. These challenges were designed to impede your progress in life and to make reaching your ultimate goals seem unattainable.

You may encounter barriers of all kinds such as sickness, sorrows and suffering, financial crises, family crises, loss of a job, spiritual battles and the like ... but there is hope! There is a way to conquer your challenges and triumph in this life, despite how severe your trial or temptation. Your faith will be tested but you must not give up, you must stay in the fight!

In the Bible, Job stands out as one of the persons who endured great tragedy and trials. He was an upright and integral man and so the Lord *allowed* satan to test him. *(Job 1:6-12)* You must understand that whenever you are going through trials and temptations, it is because

God is allowing your faith to be tested. He wants your faith to be refined like gold that has been purified. He wants your life to be a testimony of His grace and mercy, of His providence and provisions. Like any proud father, He wants to be able to say of you, *"There goes my child and I am proud of him/her!"*

Do not lose hope in the middle of your trials and temptations. Seek God, persevere, and keep pushing, pressing and prevailing until you gain the victory over your situation. I understand exactly where you are. I write from my own personal experiences. There was a season very early in my life when God was trying to get my attention. His ultimate plan for my life was full time Ministry but I could not see it and did not want to see it.

Actually, like Jonah and so many of you, I ran from the call of God on my life. However, God has a way of getting us where He wants us. He may have to design an entire situation to allow us to be still and seek Him so that He can speak into our lives. God may not use great whales to harness our attention but He may use the trials of life.

The methods may have changed but the message remains the same. God wants to get your attention in the midst of the "testing of your faith." If you are experiencing any kind of challenge or warfare and you are in God, I guarantee you can handle it and you will make it out!

"There hath no temptation taken you but such as is common to man: but God is faithful, who will not suffer you to be tempted above that ye are able; but will with the temptation also make a way to escape, that ye may be able to bear it."
(1 Corinthians 10:13)

When you experience trials, tests and temptations, God will give you the strength to endure and also provide a way to escape. Again, His purpose is being fulfilled in our lives through the testing of our faith and as we experience and overcome temptations. *When we are able to conqueror temptations and trials:*

a. We become more like Christ "... *Til Christ be formed in us" (Galatians 4:19)*

b. We become much stronger, more steadfast, enduring and persevering

"Be strong in the Lord and the power of his might..." (Ephesians 6:10)

"Be ye steadfast, immovable, always abounding in the work of the Lord..." (1 Corinthians 15:58)

"Fight the good fight of faith...."
(1 Timothy 6:12)

"Blessed is the man that endureth temptation: for when he is tried, he shall receive the crown of life, which the Lord hath promised to them that love him." (James 1:12)

c. We become a dynamic witness to all those who see us. We demonstrate not only that Jesus is alive in our lives, but also the power of God.

"But ye shall receive power, after that the Holy Ghost is come upon you: and ye shall be witnesses unto me …." (Acts 1:8)

GRACE

I believe grace covers all. Grace is God's unmerited favor. You cannot buy it and you do not have to earn it. Grace has already been given to you through the blood of Jesus Christ. Therefore, if you have accepted Christ as Lord of your life then you have accepted grace – grace is Jesus.

"My grace is sufficient for you and my strength is made perfect in weakness …"
(2 Corinthians 12:9)

Regardless of what you go through in life, God has extended His grace to you. You will overcome because grace has already overcome for you.

You may be down but you are not out. In the game of baseball, there are a total of three strikes allowed and then you are considered out. In professional basketball, you are allowed six fouls before you are fouled out of the game. In the sport of Boxing, if you are knocked down and do not get back up after a ten count, you are considered out. You may hear your enemies saying that you are finished and it is over for you, but just when they are about to say, "... − 8 − 9 − 10 ... you're out!" I hear another voice say *"Hold it right there! It's not over yet. I have the final say!"* This is the voice of the Holy Spirit.

No-one has the right to pronounce a judgment or sentence on you. God always has the final say and *it ain't over until God says it's over*. Keep fighting!

"The joy of the Lord is your strength"
(Nehemiah 8:10)

"LEADING WHILE BLEEDING"

As a child of God, you will encounter challenges, temptations and trials. Those in the pulpit are not exempt from seasons of trials, neither are those who are in the pews. However, more times than naught, it is the person in the pew whose trials are highlighted. You may be in a position of servant leadership in your local assembly as leader/coordinator of various ministries such as Christian Education, Media & Publications, Hospitality, Protocol, and The Fine Arts, etc.

As a result of being in such positions, you will experience some levels of warfare. This warfare may come from without or from within.

"AS YOU LEAD YOU MAY BLEED!"

You will go through situations where you may become wounded in battle. My wife, Prophetess Mattie Nottage, in her best-selling book, *Breaking the Chains from Worship to Warfare addresses five primary challenges that the believer faces on a daily basis:*

- They do not know the enemy they are fighting
- They do not know how to fight
- They do not know how to deal with the wounded
- They do not know how to heal themselves
- They do not understand their kingdom assignment

If the body of Christ would get to the point of being *"master"* of these areas then we would not have so many casualties. We would not have so many persons ready to retreat and surrender when faced with fiery trials, neither would there be persons who faint and quit because they are leaders and they are hurting. The church is supposed to be a hospital for sick people. If you cannot come to the church or your brothers and sisters in Christ when you are in crisis, then that is a sad predicament to be in. The Bible declares in *Galatians 6:2* that we are to,

> *"Bear ye one another's burdens, and so fulfill the law of Christ."*

Do not stop serving in your local assembly and serving your leaders because you are hurting or going through some hard times. The things that you are experiencing in your life may not be good right now, but that is not an excuse for you to stop doing what *God* has called you to do. If you sit down and do nothing then you will get nothing.

When I was building my last house, I needed steel for the foundation. From the beginning of the project, I needed the property to be cleared and cleaned but I did not have the finances at the time. I went to several persons until I found someone who would do it for me. I showed the gentleman the property and by the next day it was cleared, without any prior arrangements and or monies exchanging hands. He said to me, "When you get the money, you can pay me." If you push hard enough, things will happen for you. *Stop making excuses!*

Next, I needed the foundation dug and the same gentleman who cleared the property came back without being paid and dug the foundation. Do not look at your situation the way it is presently. Stop looking at what you can see! You have to train yourself to focus on what God said and is saying. Step out in faith and trust Him, even when you are hurting, confused and/or in the middle of trials.

You must understand that as you are doing God's work, whether as an usher or Sunday School teacher, you may have challenging situations going on in your life, but you cannot stop functioning. God will turn your situation around - just stay faithful to what He has called you to do.

"KEEP YOUR FOCUS!"

The devil is always on the look out to try and distract and destroy God's children. He is relentless and will not give up. He will keep coming after you as long as you are alive and serving God. In **1 Peter 5:8-9** the Word of God warns,

> *[8]Be sober, be vigilant; because your adversary the devil, as a roaring lion, walketh about, seeking whom he may devour:*

⁹Whom resist steadfast in the faith, knowing that the same afflictions are accomplished in your brethren that are in the world

Even when you get close to God, the devil will still seek to come after you. If he cannot get you, he will come after those close to you, such as your spouse, children and good friends. The enemy sometimes uses people to distract you. His goal is not just to stop you from praying. He desires to stop you from believing God and frustrate you right out of your kingdom assignment.

"Be not ignorant of satan's devices...."
(2 Corinthians 2:11)

"...but understand what the will of the Lord is..." (Ephesians 5:17)

The battle is not yours to fight on your own. Your assignment is to resist the devil. We have an advocate, who is Jesus. He does battle for us. You must keep your faith strong, waging war, especially warfaring against the enemy that fights within your mind.

³For though we walk in the flesh, we do not war after the flesh:

[4](For the weapons of our warfare are not carnal, but mighty through God to the pulling down of strong holds;)

[5]Casting down imaginations, and every high thing that exalteth itself against the knowledge of God, and bringing into captivity every thought to the obedience of Christ;

[6]And having in a readiness to revenge all disobedience, when your obedience is fulfilled (2 Corinthians 10:3-6)

You must learn to do battle against your enemy, engaging weapons of steadfast and prevailing prayer, diligent study of the word of God, fasting, sowing into the work of the Kingdom, worship, and more.

Ideally, we know how to fight or contend for earthly or material things but we must learn how to fight in the Spirit. You must begin to aim your ammunition at the enemy, especially when you are hurting, and not at your brothers and sisters.

THE FATE OF THE HURTING AND WOUNDED

Churches are filled with people who are hurting or going through dilemmas in their lives. Pastors, deacons, ushers and even the praise team singers have a mandate to usher people into God's presence, telling them to lift their hands, even while they themselves are hurting.

It does not matter who you are, at some point in your life you will go through something painful. That does not mean that you stop what you are doing. The Bible says that when Job found out that all his family had died, his cattle destroyed and he had lost everything, he still bowed and worshipped *(Job 1:20)*.

The church today must get the mindset that despite what the devil throws against us, we will still praise and worship God. Serving God should not depend on our feelings. We should not be circumstantial or "fair weather" Christians. Job came to the conclusion in the book of **Job 1:21**, that regardless of his position, the name of the Lord is worthy to be blessed. Moreover, even when the Lord allows something to be taken, He is getting ready to promote you and give you something even better. You may be hurting but hold on, the best is yet to come.

"Though he slay me, yet will I trust in him: but I will maintain mine own ways before him." (Job 13:15)

NOT QUITTING IN THE WAR ZONE!

You are in a war but you have to fight to survive. You have to fight for every prophecy that was spoken over your life, waging a full-fledged war to maintain your victory. This means you will have to strategize, getting up early and binding the devil, praying with all types of prayers, commanding your morning.

"My voice shalt thou hear in the morning, O LORD; in the morning will I direct my prayer unto thee, and will look up" (Psalm 5:3)

"O God, thou art my God; early will I seek thee..." (Psalm 63;1)

Can you imagine if every time your house came under an attack, you left? Your enemies would soon figure out a way to keep you out. Jesus said, Behold, I give you keys of the kingdom and according to *Matthew 18:18,*

> *[18] Verily I say unto you, Whatsoever ye shall bind on earth shall be bound in heaven: and whatsoever ye shall loose on earth shall be loosed in heaven.*

The keys represent spiritual authority and power. God has given you power over all power of the enemy.

> *"Behold, I give unto you power to tread on serpents and scorpions, and over all the power of the enemy: and nothing shall by any means hurt you." (Luke 10:19)*

This means that you are well protected from any attack that the enemy can launch against you. Your victory is sure as you adorn your spiritual armour which is:
1) The helmet of salvation
2) The sword of the Spirit which is the word of God
3) The breastplate of living righteously
4) Walking in the ways of peace
5) Girded and living a life of truth

6) The shield of faith whereby you will block and destroy the fiery darts and onslaught of the wicked.

WORRYING PROFITS NOTHING

In the book of **1 Peter 5:7**, God admonishes us to cast our cares upon Him. Worrying and carrying cares leads to stress. Stress is a killer! It weighs you down. You become stressed out because you carry your burdens and all of the situations that you are confronted with daily.

"Do Not Carry Your Cares But Cast Them!"

Stress will cause you to have a heart attack. You must learn to forgive, release and let go. If somebody has hurt you, do not hold it in your heart. The weight of that care will bring stress on your life, cast it off of you and on to Jesus! Do not be afraid to put things in God's hands.

According to *James 4:7-8,* we can keep resisting the devil. *To resist* means *to oppose or fight off.* Resistance has to start in the mind and not be initiated when something starts to materialize. The devil launches his initial attacks in your mind. This is where the battle begins, before anything manifests, it starts off as a thought. So again, you must bring every thought captive to the mindset of Christ. *(2 Corinthians 10:5)*

Further, you resist the devil by drawing near to God. It does not exempt you from temptation but, it gives you power to resist or withstand the temptation. If you are going through and you are in God and He allows it, this means that He has confidence in you that you are able to bear it. *(1 Corinthians 10:13.)*

God will bring you out and you will not come out empty. You will be able to maintain and sustain the place where He is carrying you. Hold on to God, allow Him to direct your paths *(Proverbs 3:5-6)* and show you how to get out. Hold on until you come forth as pure gold!

A FIRM FOUNDATION

God is doing a new thing and preparing you for the absolute best which is to come. Do not move out of position. You are on a firm foundation. According to *1 Peter 5:10,* after you have suffered a while, God will *make you perfect, stablish, strengthen, settle you.*

I have had various unforgettable, life-threatening experiences which, at the moment, made me feel as though I was hanging over a cliff. but God rescued me. Everything that could be shaken was shaken in my life, including my marriage, my money and material possessions. I had to make a decision to stay in faith, keep on fighting or "jump overboard."

"God has a way to get you out of your hurt. However, you cannot drop your assignment because of what you are going through."

Many times I had to find a way to rise above the situations and the storm while continuing to do what God had called me to do. I discovered that your blessing is in your pressing and the more you continue to push your way through, you will eventually get to the place where God wants you to be.

Take some time to fight in the realm of the spirit, you will find peace in the presence of Almighty God.

PREPARATION

What you are going through is only preparation. Something great is coming out of it and you will laugh again. Once again remember, failure is not final and everything around you is subject to change for your good. Your preparation season is a necessary stop on your journey to ensure that you are ready to embrace your final destination.

What you are seeing now is temporary as revealed in *2 Corinthians 4:18.* Do not make life-altering decisions while you are hurting, because more than likely; you will not make wise choices. Bear down and push again. Like a woman in labor; you will soon forget your pain once you have given birth to your dream. *(Romans 8:14)*

ELEVATION

From rejection comes elevation. You cannot see it now but God is preparing you for something great. When the hand of God is upon your life, yet still you will rise. It is not over until God says it is over.

Man's stopping point is God's starting point. You have to see the big picture. If you could only see in the realm of the Spirit, God is working it out and you shall overcome every test, trial and temptation.

CHAPTER 3

TRUSTING GOD

DEALING WITH ADVERSITY

Several years ago I preached a message entitled *"Hope against Hope."* At that time, that series was considered one the greatest messages I had ever preached and it eventually became one of my best sellers as many peoples' lives were blessed by it.

Looking back from then to now, I realize that God had given me that word because I lived it. I had gone through so many adversities in life that I could write a book. (Which I am doing right now!)

An adversity may be defined as **an unfortunate event, incident or hardship.** Well, I have seen a whole lot of all of the above; from losing my business, my home, cars, thousands and thousands of dollars in investment projects and at one point almost losing my family.

It was during these trying times in my life that I came to understand that there is a difference between saying you *have* faith and actually *trusting* God in spite of what you are going through.

Faith is the confidence that you have in God for that which you are hoping for. But when you have fasted, prayed and cried all night and the answer still is not there what do you do? " *You trust God!"*

Trusting God in my opinion goes beyond just *saying* you have faith. Trust is having all odds stacked against you but standing strong and holding on to whatever God has told you. It is to be resolute, with boldness and confidence, that He is working all things for your good.

"Faithful is He that has promised..." (Hebrews 10:23),

" ... for yet a little while and He that shall come will come and shall not tarry" (Hebrews 10:37)

Adversities will come but God is always looking to show Himself strong in the midst of those who will hold on and trust in Him. Satan is our archenemy and even though you may not see him, he uses people and tumultuous events to challenge your faith in an effort to discourage you.

"Be sober, be vigilant for your adversary the devil walketh about seeking whom he may devour, whom resist stedfast." (1 Peter 5: 8)

It is the people who truly trust God and are holding firm to His promises that are the people who are endowed with power. These are the people who are steadfast, immovable and resolute in their faith. God surrounds these people with divine protection that causes them to rise above every storm and calamity.

"They that trust in the Lord shall be as Mount Zion which cannot be removed, but abideth forever. As the mountains are round about Jerusalem, so the Lord is round about His people from henceforth even forever." (Psalm 125:1)

STRESSED OUT!

There were times that I felt like quitting. Certainly, I cannot count the numerous times I felt like giving up. There were nights I felt as though I was losing my mind. I could hardly sleep just thinking about what was going to happen if I did not get the monies to pay a bill or meet a deadline.

I used to be so "stressed out" it was unbelievable. My blood pressure was off the scale and I was also plagued with migraine headaches. Things would get so bad that people would be talking to me and I would disappear into a deep day dream, cleaning my nails right in-front of them.

It got really bad and I knew at some point I had to catch myself and start trusting God beyond my circumstances.

THE DAY MY LIFE CHANGED

I felt like a hypocrite somewhat. I was telling everyone to have faith in God and there I was living in "Stress Village." Everyone that knew me knows me as a "man of faith." I seldom worried about anything and could almost boast in the fact that I wore problems like a "loose garment."

I had to ask myself, "When did all of this happen? When did I become "stressed"? I was not sure when I opened that door to frustration, but I can certainly tell you the day I closed the door and made a decision to change my life.

I needed over a quarter of a million dollars. I was going through a major stormy season again. This new storm was unlike any other storm I had ever experienced. My entire life was jolted out of position and we found ourselves (my wife and our three kids) living on the streets in our old Mitsubishi Coupe with nowhere to go. This was very humiliating and not to mention, painful to bear. We had no monies, no food and nowhere to go. We could hardly afford a cheap motel.

I had no one to turn to but God; trusting Him as my refuge and hiding place. I remembered the Spirit of God speaking to me and saying five simple words, *"Trust me, I'm with you."* After hearing those comforting words I thought for sure things were going to change and get better, instantly. Not only did they not get better, they got progressively worse.

I became angry with every "faith" teacher that was on television. However, I knew that if I was going to survive this storm I had to do something I had never done before. I decided to activate every spiritual principle I had ever learnt. Every day I got up I would declare the word to myself, to my wife and kids. Every day I told them that today was the day that God was going to work a miracle for us. Every day I worshipped and found something that I could give to someone in order to be a blessing.

I began moving myself from being angry to giving God praise and worship all day and all night. Something strange began happening. People started coming to me for prayers regarding their problems. I would pray the prayer of faith and watched God work supernatural miracles right before my eyes.

Word of what God was doing began to spread everywhere. I became so consumed with helping others with their problems that I totally forgot about my own.

That was the day my life changed. I did not realize it until we were having dinner one evening and one of my kids said, "Dad, thank God we are not out on the streets anymore." It was true. God had done just what He had promised. He seemed to have waited until I took the focus off of my own situation and reached out to help someone else.

"Don't Quit! God may be using your circumstances to bring healing and deliverance to someone else.

BY THIS TIME TOMORROW

Can you imagine the unbelievable horror of living a normal, successful life; working hard every day only to wake up one morning and discover that you have been diagnosed with a chronic disease? You can no longer work and suddenly everything you own begins to slip away from you. You are suddenly in jeopardy of losing everything - your house, car, family – you suddenly find yourself in a debilitating position and locked out of society.

THE SPIRIT OF LEPROSY

In the book of **2 Kings 7**, we find the story of four men who had one thing in common – they were lepers. Just a few months prior, they all worked good jobs, went to church and took care of their families. However, some unforeseen circumstance or sudden tragedy brought each of these men to a point of destitution, rejection, despair and ultimate embarrassment; left for dead and locked out of the city. Each day, their leprosy grew worse as tumors and sores quickly covered them from head to toe.

Not only were the lepers experiencing hardship outside the gates of the city – but their entire city was experiencing a famine that was never seen before. The king and all of his citizens were perplexed as there seemed to be no hope. *These four lepers had several odds against them:*

- They were lepers
- They were deemed unclean
- They lost all of their possessions and became poor.
- They were cast out of the city.
- They were left to die.

They had no idea what was taking place in their city. All they knew was that there was a famine. When things
are sometimes at their worse, God will always raise up a prophet to speak a word. Elisha was a man of faith and power. He already knew that whatever he spoke, God would bring to pass. In fact, he had already proven this mighty God so many times Elisha had no doubt in his mind that He would show up in the midst of the famine. The Word of God lets us know,

> *"Elisha stood in the courtyard before the king and all the people and prophesied, Then Elisha said, Hear ye the word of the LORD; Thus saith the LORD, <u>Tomorrow about this time</u> shall a measure of fine flour be sold for a shekel, and two measures of barley for a shekel, in the gate of Samaria." (2 Kings 7:1)*

The lepers had no idea that God had used Elisha to prophecy that within twenty four hours the famine would be over. They (the lepers) were locked out of their city and knew that there was only one way to survive.

Elisha spoke in faith with boldness. One of the king's armour bearers doubted the prophetic word and laughed stating that there was no way such a miracle could be performed – even if there were windows in heaven.

Elisha was somewhat enraged by the doubtful words of the armour bearer and told him that he would surely see the prophetic word come to pass but he will not enjoy any of the blessings that were coming.

"Faith in God is what brings your miracle into manifestation. Doubt will only bring death and destruction."

The four lepers had no idea of what was being spoken in their city. The only thing they knew is that they were cold, sick, hungry and about to die. They had to make a decision – either they would stay where they were and die, holding on to the gate of their city or they would turn around and go into a nearby city (Syria) in search of food. They chose to take a chance – risking everything.

Because they were willing to risk everything and trust solely in God – God favored them. As they walked into the Syrian camp, the Spirit of God caused their feet to sound like a mighty army that was coming to attack. For fear of losing their lives, the Syrians abandoned their tents, leaving all of their clothes, food, silver and gold behind. The lepers could not believe their eyes as they entered the recently vacated tents. They ate to their hearts content and were able to exchange their rags for riches – praising God for the sudden turn in their misfortune. The next day they told the king about the miraculous blessing they received. The wheat, barley, and the oil were available for distribution at the gate. The entire city was so overwhelmed by their next day miracle that in their haste for the food, they trampled and killed the king's armourbearer.

It does not matter how bad things look today in your life. God is a God of the supernatural. He can work a miracle for you – *"by this time tomorrow."*

God honors His word above His name and if God has ever spoken anything to you, you can depend on Him and that word to come to pass. He is able to turn your life around and give you a miracle by this same time tomorrow. You are reading this now, and by this time tomorrow your circumstances can be totally changed! Like the lepers, you must just step out in faith and act.

FAITH IS NOW AND NOW IS FAITH!

Faith is a lifestyle! The way you live your life is a clear indication of where your faith lies. Faith is also one of the most powerful words in the universe, but it is one that is most misunderstood. For the most part, people tend to see faith as something that has to do with your future only. However, what many fail to realize is that you have to have faith for the "now" or better, for the present.

You need faith to make right decisions and choices for present circumstances and situations so that you are ensured a prosperous future. In **Hebrews 11:1,** the Word of God states that,

"Now faith is the substance of things hoped for, the evidence of things not seen."

Now faith is the *title-deed* of all of the things that we anticipate and expect in our future. Our faith or consistent belief is the thing that brings these things into manifestation. As you add strategic works to what you believe, step by step you begin to demonstrate those things that were once in your hearts and minds as only visions, dreams or ideas.

In **Romans 4:17**, the Word of God tells us how God is able to call those things that be not, as though they were. The very nature of God is to make things happen. God, as Elohim, is never short on resources or supply. He is the Source of all things so whatever He needs, He speaks into existence. This is the same attribute that we, as the people of God can walk in. **(Mark 11:22 – 24)**

"Now Faith" never looks at the circumstances. It laughs at impossibilities and never wavers at the promises of God. This type of faith sees God instead of the situation. So even if it seems as though you have failed, and nothing is working, faith says, "It's not over yet! I have to persevere! I have to get back in the fight!"

"Faith is a verb, it denotes action. Faith is an action word. You must refuse to sit and die in your circumstances. Faith is a lifestyle - you must exercise it every day."

If the doctors diagnosed you with a disease, that may be a fact, but faith and truth says, *"By His stripes I am healed!"* Your creditors may be calling. Your bank account may be in "the red" but the word of God says that *you are blessed; you are a lender and not a borrower!* Your children may be acting contrary now but the word says that when you *train up a child in the way he should go, when he is old he will not depart from it!* Your marriage may be on the rocks, even hanging over the cliff but the word says, *marriage is honorable ... what God has joined together no man can put asunder.*

By this time tomorrow, God can transform your life. You can go from broke to blessed, sick to being healed and made whole. God can perform miracles if you just believe and step out in faith and obedience. Just ask the widow woman in 2Kings 4 or the Shunamite woman in the book of 1 Kings 17. Their lives were changed in one day.

These accounts in the Bible are not fairy tales or fictitious. God did it back then and He can do it now. You may need to ask, "What is hindering me from experiencing my *"by this time tomorrow"* blessings? It is simply a matter of faith. Bind the spirits of fear and doubt and walk in your season of "now faith."

> *"For God hath not given us the spirit of fear; but of power, and of love, and of a sound mind ..."*
> *(2 Timothy 1:7)*

CHAPTER 4

WHAT GOD HAS FOR YOU...

"I'LL NEVER BE A SLAVE AGAIN!"

"*Slave*" is a word that does not carry positive connotations. For many individuals it is associated with disgrace, shame and pain. By definition, *a slave is somebody who is forced to work for someone else for no payment and is regarded as the property of that person; somebody who is dominated by someone or by a system.*

On the other hand, the Bible admonishes us to be **servants,** translated **slaves** for Christ. (*1 Peter 2:16, Galatians 1:10, 1 Corinthians 7:21-22*). This is the type of "*slavery*" we should attain to.

Slavery has been abolished but many persons are still walking around enslaved. They are slaves in their minds and are operating with a defeatist mentality. This can be true, even of some Christians.

The mind is a battle field and this is why the word instructs us to *"pull down strong holds and cast down imaginations in the mind" (2 Corinthians 10:3-6)*

"*Strongholds represent negative belief systems that may govern an individual, groups of people, small communities or even* entire nations. Strongholds are agents assigned to keep you in bondage. They usually affect individuals by attacking their mind or emotions with false arguments, which seek to spiritually demobilize and paralyze their thought patterns. Remember, the battlefield is in the mind. (pp 219-220 *Breaking the Chains–From Worship to Warfare.*)

"Strongholds are resistant to change and drastic measures should be taken in prayer to diminish them."

BATTLEFIELD OF THE MIND

Most people do not recognize when they are enslaved or in bondage. The absence of physical chains or cords may mislead them into a sense of false reality; the fact that they find themselves struggling year after year with some of the same issues or demons is an indication that there is a spiritual warfare going on in their mind.

It is in the mind that some of your greatest battles take place. It is there where the enemy attacks the most. He suggests negative thoughts to you. Your thoughts become words, your words produce actions and your actions will denote your lifestyle.

"As a man thinketh in his heart, so is he."
(Proverbs 23:7)

You can be enslaved mentally if you live with a defeatist mentality. This mindset causes you to believe that you cannot succeed or become anything in life. This disposition may be as a result of the negative seeds that were sown into your spirit from your childhood. As you grow, these seeds are watered by spirits of low self esteem, fear and doubt.

As you become an adult, you will begin to notice various trends of behaviors. Words are so powerful, as the Bible declares that *death and life are in the power of the tongue....Proverbs 18:21.* We must use words that encourage and not injure, words that inspire and not inflict. Learn to speak blessings and not cursing. You must use your mouth to speak life, especially over your children "emancipating yourselves from mental slavery."

[1]"I beseech you therefore, brethren, by the mercies of God, that ye present your bodies a living sacrifice, holy, acceptable unto God, which is your reasonable service."

[2]"And be not conformed to this world: but be ye transformed by the renewing of your mind, that ye may prove what is that good, and acceptable, and perfect, will of God" (Romans 12:1,2)

Begin to renew and reprogram your mind so that you will begin thinking the way God thinks. Eventually, every stronghold will be destroyed and you would have birthed a new mind that is programmed to win.

MY EMANCIPATION DAY

After graduating from high school I started working in water sports. The monies were coming in so fast that I could not believe what I was pulling in daily for the company.

Although I was working for the company and making a lot of money, I knew within myself that I could one day do this for myself. I worked hard every day in the scorching sun, sacrificing lunch breaks and vacation. I worked hard even during storms and bad weather, as long as tourists wanted a boat ride or parasail ride, I was willing to do it. I was extremely determined to make something of my life and was prepared to do whatever it took. I was later able to save enough monies to purchase my own boat and equipment. I became an Entrepreneur.

This was one of the happiest days of my life. Wow! God was blessing me beyond measure. Right away I began strategizing and planning what I wanted to do. The first thing I did was built a home for my wife and children. I bought a duplex apartment and purchased a brand new car all within one year.

SOMETHING WENT VERY WRONG

We were now making great strides and I began feeling like a millionaire. However, I began losing my focus and by the following summer my whole world seemed to have come crashing down.

Whenever you take your eyes off of God and become caught up in materialism or personal gain you will fall. I realized that I made a big mistake being distracted cost me a hefty penalty. Everything began falling apart. My boat sank and all of my equipment was damaged. My insurance company took days to send an agent to inspect my boat which was partially submerged.

By the time they finally came, my boat had been totally damaged and they did not want to honor the claim and pay us out. I had to choose either to stay there or walk away. I chose to walk away from the beach leaving prospects of a multi-million dollar business behind. I ended up home without a job and no money for several months.

Everything was under a severe attack and I did not know where to turn. After several months, I finally found a job at a wholesale company selling juice and snack foods. They were only willing to pay me one hundred and fifty dollars ($150.00) per week because it was a new route they were giving me and they had very low expectations of it producing anything.

Well, that is all I needed to hear and could not wait to get started. I worked six days a week and lots of over time just to get new customers and set up a totally new route. Within two weeks I had miraculously surpassed the company's sales record developing a portfolio of faithful cash paying customers – by the grace of God. The entire management team was surprised, shocked and in total amazement. My new customers were tripling their orders and my sale quota was breaking records and going beyond all barriers.

GOOD THINGS "SOMETIMES" COME TO AN END

I continued excelling, increasing my sales target each week. Eventually, the company gave me two new workers to train. I was told that they were the owners' son and nephew. I felt honored, only to discover three months later before my probation had ended, that my new "super great" job was being snatched from beneath me. I was called into a meeting and told my services were no longer needed. My truck and new route were then given to the young men that I had trained. I was not given any explanations, no apology, and no severance – just a *cold*, "You're no longer needed!"

I could not believe my ears for what I was hearing and certainly could not believe my eyes for what I was seeing. I spent over three months working around the clock building that entire route, and then I watched it taken right out of my hands. I was devastated and felt totally crushed by a system I had no control over. After all, it was *their* business, *their* son, *their* nephew and not to mention *their* new customers.

I surrendered the truck keys and began walking towards the front gate. That was the longest walk of my entire life, I will never forget it. Tears were streaming down my face. I was embarrassed and felt like a failure. My wife picked me up that day and she kept asking me, "What had happened?" I could not talk. Eventually, I muttered twenty (20) words,

"I'll never be a slave again and I will never work a single day for another man for the rest of my life."

I repeated it and kept repeating it...until I became convinced and it was indelibly marked in my spirit.

A SET BACK OR A SET UP?

Those twenty words ...

"I'll never be a slave again and I will never work a single day for another man for the rest of my life"

... became the driving motivation to my road of freedom and I made a decision from that very moment, that I was not sending out another resume or job application. I began seeking the face of God day and night and this time I only wanted His will. This is what I called *"My Emancipation Day".*

God gave me the stamina and strength to overcome. I believe that maybe I had to go through that in order to get to my next level. Even though I did not realize it then, I certainly understand it now that this truly was a set up and not a setback, as I had originally thought. He was setting me up for something far greater than I could ever imagine.

At this level, you must operate in total faith, trusting God to perform His will in your life. After all, what God has for you, it is for you!

> *"And we know that all things work together for good to them that love God, to them who are the called according to his purpose."*
> *(Romans 8:28)*

WHAT GOD HAS FOR YOU–IT IS FOR YOU!

"But they that wait upon the LORD shall renew their strength; they shall mount up with wings as eagles; they shall run, and not be weary; and they shall walk, and not faint." (Isaiah 40:31)

The eagle is a majestic creature. He soars high in the heavens and seems to glide effortlessly, even in the midst of storms. When I think of how the eagles' wings have been designed with such ingenuity by Almighty God, I consider them to be parables of our "*wings of faith*".

It takes faith to seek and trust God. Trusting and believing God is a condition of the heart. According to **Hebrews 11:6**,

> *"For anyone who comes to God must first believe that He is (or that He exists) and that He is a Rewarder of them that diligently seek Him."*

And just like the eagle; once you extend your faith towards Him, the wind of the Holy Spirit will lift you into His presence. Once you have entered the center of God's divine will He begins to unveil His promises to you.

> *"In His presence there is fullness of joy and at His right hand there are pleasures evermore." (Psalm 16:11)*

He instructs you through faith-building experiences and lessons which teach you, how to rise above difficult circumstances, challenges and hindrances in your life. By the power of the Holy Spirit, you can learn how to rise to even higher dimensions of faith, gaining the Father's perspective and spiritual wisdom on what is above.

"The soul of the diligent shall be made fat ..."
(Proverbs 13:4)

INTENSIFY YOUR SEEK

Seek God for His divine will and purpose for your life, for more of His presence and most of all - His anointing. Seek Him and draw closer to Him in order to gain a greater understanding of the mysteries of the kingdom.

After I lost my job, I was compelled to seek God because I did not have a choice. You do not have to wait until tragedy hits your life before you go after God; seek Him willingly, now.

"For the LORD God is a sun and shield: the LORD will give grace and glory: no good thing will he withhold from them that walk uprightly" (Psalms 84:11)

Every promise that God has ever made to you, He will perform it.

God is not a man, that he should lie; neither the son of man, that he should repent: hath he said, and shall he not do it? or hath he spoken, and shall he not make it good? (Numbers 23:19)

It does not matter how your situation may look right now. God said, "Before the foundations of the earth, He knew you." When you were in your mother's belly, He called you.

"DON'T RUN!"

Initially, I tried to run from the calling on my life for full time ministry. I discovered that trying to run from God is a waste of time. I ended up going through a series of loop holes and pitfalls only to end right back where He wanted me.

You are so special to Him that He knows every strand of hair on your head **(Matthew 10:30)**. In fact He knows your uprising and your down-setting. It makes no sense running. It is quite easier to stop and begin doing whatever it is He has called you to do. No more running! What God has for you – it is for you!

"Heaven and earth shall pass away, but my words shall not pass away" (Matthew 24:35)

- *No weapon formed against you shall prosper!*
- *No good thing will He withhold from you!*

- *What God has for you – it is for you!*

ANOINTED TO BE KING

I can vividly remember being in Sunday school as a young boy and hearing Bible stories about Jonah in the belly of a whale, Jesus feeding the five thousand and even the stories of David.

The life of King David has always impressed me; how that from a child, he was used by God to accomplish many feats. As a shepherd boy David killed a lion and a bear and, ultimately killed Goliath.   None of these encounters were easy victories.   Nevertheless, they positioned him as a teenager to be anointed as the future king over Israel.

> *"And the LORD said unto Samuel, How long wilt thou mourn for Saul, seeing I have rejected him from reigning over Israel? fill thine horn with oil, and go, I will send thee to Jesse the Bethlehemite: for I have provided me a king among his sons.*
>
> *[10] Again, Jesse made seven of his sons to pass before Samuel. And Samuel said unto Jesse, The LORD hath not chosen these.*

[11]And Samuel said unto Jesse, Are here all thy children? And he said, There remaineth yet the youngest, and, behold, he keepeth the sheep. And Samuel said unto Jesse, Send and fetch him: for we will not sit down till he come hither.

[12]And he sent, and brought him in. Now he was ruddy, and withal of a beautiful countenance, and goodly to look to. And the LORD said, Arise, anoint him: for this is he.

[13]Then Samuel took the horn of oil, and anointed him in the midst of his brethren: and the Spirit of the LORD came upon David from that day forward. So Samuel rose up, and went to Ramah." (1 Samuel 16)

THE PROCESS BEFORE THE PALACE

Even as a young man with the anointing of God smeared on his life, David still went through many tests and trials. In fact, he spent many years before sitting on the throne, running from Saul. Sometimes in life even though God anoints you for a particular blessing, you may have to go through hills and valleys, fighting for your life before getting there.

David made many mistakes; on his way to the palace and even while he was king. He was an adulterer and a murderer when, during his reign, he had Uriah killed and took his wife, Bathsheba. However, he was also a worshipper. He knew how to find forgiveness and his way back to the presence of God.

You may also fall down and make mistakes on your way to destiny. Don't quit! Find the courage to pick yourself up, brush yourself off, square your shoulders and repent. Keep moving forward!

David went through a process of being broken. The Holy Spirit wanted him to remain humble and yielded totally to His will.

[1]Have mercy upon me, O God, according to thy loving kindness: according unto the multitude of thy tender mercies blot out my transgressions.

[2]Wash me thoroughly from mine iniquity, and cleanse me from my sin.

[3]For I acknowledge my transgressions: and my sin is ever before me. (Psalm 51:1-3)

Now that you have repented, move forward, the throne awaits you.

"Thou anointest my head with oil..." *(Psalm 23)*

DESPERATE TO STAY IN THE FIGHT

Although he was king over Israel, David was still desperate to stay in the will of God. This desperation kept him on the altar of prayer. Whenever he made mistakes, he was always willing to find God in true repentance. *This is the mark of a man who is desperate to stay in the fight.*

His journey from a shepherd boy to one of the greatest kings of Israel was marked with much controversy and calamity, but also victory and triumph. He always refused to be counted out and he refused to accept defeat. He was determined to be a man after God's own heart.

Do not become discouraged. God is in the midst of every one of your circumstances. He formed you in your mother's belly, according to the word, and has anointed you from a child. Stay in the fight. Do not become distracted or frustrated in the middle of your transition. You will become "*king.*" You will become a homeowner, business owner, and successful parent. You will graduate from high school, college or university. Your marriage will work. You will fulfill your dreams, visions and ideas. You will fulfill your kingdom assignment. You will be all that God has called and created you to be, in the mighty name of Jesus.

CHAPTER 5

FAITH, POWER & GLORY

A MEASURE OF FAITH

Too many people give up, before even making an effort to try again. **Romans 12:3**, states that each one of us is given a measure of faith. In other words, regardless of who you are or where you have come from, God has deposited faith in you. He has given you the ability to believe and have confidence to accomplish whatever you so desire.

"Having faith is the assurance (the confirmation, the title deed) of the things you are hoping for, being the proof of things you do not see and the conviction of their reality (faith) perceiving as real, fact, what is not revealed to your senses." (Hebrews 11:1 AMP)

Faith therefore is your guarantee that you will achieve your desired results, by God's grace, even though you do not see it as yet with your physical eyes.

I SEE A CLOUD

Elijah the prophet was a man just like you and I. In the book of **1 Kings 18:2**, there was a severe drought for over three years in the land of Samaria. Elijah stood on the mountain and prophesied that the rain was coming.

He repeatedly sent his servant to look at the clouds from which the rain would come. Elijah kept insisting that the clouds were there and that the rain was coming. Eventually the servant noticed that there was a cloud the size of a man's fist.

On that same day, the heavens opened and brought forth rain. God sent a supernatural down pour because Elijah had supernatural expectations.

MOUNTAIN MOVING FAITH

"... If ye have faith as a grain of mustard seed, ye shall say unto this mountain, Remove hence to yonder place; and it shall remove; and nothing shall be impossible unto you." (Matthew 17:20)

Mountains represent a high or fortified place. Scientists say that it takes millions of years for a mountain to form. The Himalayas took 40 million years to reach its present height and is still growing. Mountains do not move easily. It takes the God kind of faith to move them.

Regardless of how big or how strong your situation appears to be, faith in the God of Abraham, Jacob and Isaac could move it. One drop of faith in God can reposition you from defeat to victory, from the bottom to the top.

Do not quit! Use the little measure of faith that you have to turn your situations around. You must practice your faith. You must believe in your faith. It is the substance of things hoped for *(Hebrews 11:1).*

"There is faith and then there is great faith."

No one automatically has great faith because they have faith. Your faith is based on the miracles you saw God work so many times before. Great faith goes beyond what you have seen; it does not even need a physical touch. It says to Jesus, "Only speak the word and I believe it shall be done!"

Consider the account of the centurion's servant in **Luke 7:9**. His servant was about to die, but he told Jesus to just speak the word and he knew his servant would be healed. Jesus said, "I have not found so great faith, even in Israel." *Great faith tells God what His word says* and goes home expecting to "meet the miracle". People who are not willing to quit or give up, live in a realm of supernatural expectations. They expect God to do exactly what He says-beyond all doubt.

FAITH THAT OVERCOMES

God has given us faith to accomplish divine exploits although we are sometimes limited by the weakness of our human flesh. This type of faith propels us beyond how we feel, what we think and even what we know.

"But we have this treasure in earthen vessels, that the excellency of the power may be of God, and not of us"
(2 Corinthians 4:7)

God has given us faith in order to thrust us beyond our present circumstances and experiences and into new levels of blessings and victory. This type of faith causes you to open a business in spite of limited finances; this faith causes you to believe that your marriage will work although it seems as if it is falling apart; this type of faith gives you the courage to walk out of an abusive relationship even if you have nowhere to go.

This type of faith gives you what you need to overcome every obstacle or challenges that may come your way.

CRAZY FAITH

In most situations, *"crazy faith"* is motivated by some level of desperation and or determination where we have already made up in our minds that we need a miracle from God; that we need a breakthrough – by any means necessary.

When you get to this place of desperation you are willing to try just about anything to get it. This type of faith is a "crazy, unwavering faith" where we may look crazy doing it but in the end we are truly blessed because we stepped out and did what seemed to be impossible. *It is when you get to the point where you say,*

- Lord I'm tired of the rent man calling me
- I'm tired of the mortgage man calling me
- I'm tired of barely making ends meet
- I'm tired of catching the bus
- I'm tired of living with other people

It is when you have gone beyond your own pride and even the opinions of others; where you are prepared to do whatever God tells you to do in order to breakthrough to your next level of blessing and/or miracle.

You need to start calling on Jesus, and when other people do not understand your desperation you need to continue to seek God until you get an answer or your miracle manifests. When you get His attention you need to say, *"Lord I need a miracle!"*

"If ye shall ask anything in my name, I will do it."
(John 14:14)

Whenever you really need God to move, remind Him of His word; remind Him of every promise that He ever made to you. Understand, the Spirit of God will move and respond according to your faith.

In **Mark 9:23**, the Word of God states, that *"... If thou canst believe, all things are possible to him that believeth."* If you truly believe the Word of God and what God says about you, then that thing you truly believe will become possible to you. There may be times that you have to say even as the man who was crying out on behalf of his daughter said in **Mark 9:24**,

"Lord, I believe; but help thou mine unbelief."

I believe that this man was so desperate to see his daughter healed that when he got the devastating news that she had died, he was literally pleading with Jesus to do something because his faith was failing.

Sometimes you can get to a place where you are believing God so much and for so long that any negative report can greatly challenge your faith. In those times, I believe that if you cry out to God in all honesty and sincerity, speaking the true condition of your heart – God will still respond.

Sometimes you have to get like blind Bartimaeus in Mark 10:46, who sat begging on the side of the road but when he heard that Jesus was passing by, he cried out to Him with a loud voice. Now those who were standing around, who did not understand his desperation, were telling him to be quiet. But the more the crowd tried to "hush him up" the louder his cry became. It was his cry of desperation and faith that got Jesus' attention.

How desperate are you? Are you so concerned about what others think about you that you cannot cry out to God in your time of need? You must ask yourself, "What am I willing to do to get my breakthrough?" "Am I going to allow my pride to cause me to miss out on what God has for me or am I going to do whatever it takes to get God's attention?

"WHAT WOULD YOU DO FOR A MIRACLE?"

In the book of Mark chapter 2 verses 3 and 4, four men brought their friend to Jesus. These men were so crazy and radical in their faith that when they saw the door was blocked, they went to the roof and ripped it off. Why ... because they had crazy faith! They knew that they had to get their friend to Jesus. That was their job, and once they did that they knew that God would do the rest.

I believe that their single act of compassion for a friend moved Jesus all the more to perform this miracle for them. They were not going to Jesus for their own personal benefit but they were seeking a miracle for someone else.

In **Job 10:42**, the Word of God says that when Job prayed for his friends then the Lord turned his captivity. I truly believe that that day, those four men, along with their friend all received a miracle. *"What about you, are you crazy enough?"*

"Beloved, I wish above all things that thou mayest prosper and be in health, even as thy soul prospereth."
(3 John 1:2)

God wants you to prosper. You just have to be crazy enough to believe that. You have to get to the point where you believe God for everything and all things. If you need money, a house and a car, you have to believe that God can provide all of that for you but He wants you to seek the kingdom first.

> *"Seek ye first the kingdom of God and all these things shall be added unto you."(Matthew 6:33)*

If God could put money in the mouth of a fish when the tax collector came to Peter and Jesus to collect taxes then God can supernaturally provide for you.

> *"Notwithstanding, lest we should offend them, go thou to the sea, and cast an hook, and take up the fish that first cometh up; and when thou hast opened his mouth, thou shalt find a piece of money: that take, and give unto them for me and thee." (Matthew 17:27)*

Jesus told Peter to go to the sea and the first fish he caught, he was to open its mouth and the money would be there. Just as Jesus said it that is just how it happened. Not only was the money there, but it was enough to pay the whole bill. I believe that many times we do not receive what we want from God because we are not truly asking God for what we want.

For the most part, we believe Him for some of what we need and sometimes we feel that that is all that we deserve. You must have faith to believe that God is able to provide you with *everything* that you need; for He is ready, willing and able to supply all of your needs according to His riches in glory. *(Philippians 4:19)*

Think about it – money is not usually found in a fish's mouth, but Jesus spoke it, and Peter was crazy enough to believe it. Are you crazy enough to take God at His word? Then as the Word of God says in Matthew 9:29, *"...According to your faith be it unto you."*

CHAPTER 6

THE ENEMIES OF YOUR FAITH

EXPOSING FEAR

Over the years I have come to realize that there are enemies of your faith. These enemies war against you in an effort to sabotage your journey on the road to success. Three of these rivals or enemies are: fear, pride and doubt.

The spirit of fear is a strongman the adversary sometimes uses to intimidate, demobilize and cripple your faith. Fear is a "demon of master control"; once you surrender to his vices, he grips and subjects you to his stronghold. Your mind becomes overrun by negative thoughts, frightening words and destructive innuendos. For the most part, the thing that you fear does not even exist. **All F.E.A.R. really is and can be defined as:**

FALSE EVIDENCE APPEARING REAL

The spirit of fear makes false suggestions to your mind and speaks words such as:
- Suppose you fail?
- What if people laugh at you?
- What if no-one comes?
- What if the bank says, No?
- You will never make it!
- You might as well give up!

These are all lies. The moment you open the door to FEAR, he brings an entire cadre of lying demons with him.

"For God did not give us a spirit of timidity (of cowardice, of craven and cringing and fawning fear), but [He has given us a spirit] of power and of love and of calm and well-balanced mind and discipline and self-control." (2 Timothy 1:7 amp)

I can remember when God called me to pastoral ministry. I was so afraid; I thought I was going to literally pass out. I even started hyperventilating! "Surely God was not serious!" I said to myself.

I was beating the drums at my local church, cleaning toilets, parking cars and never liked holding the microphone. Growing up there were times my tongue became heavy or what we call "tied tongue." Whenever I became afraid it became more noticeable and I had problems pronouncing some words, especially those beginning with the letters "t" and "h" or "s" and "t." I was somewhat stuck in the middle of a huge family of thirteen (13) children. I seldom wasted time trying to say much to anyone. I stayed mostly to myself.

No matter how hard I tried to escape, preachers would visit our church to minister and out of nowhere identify me and begin prophesying saying, "I see you preaching the gospel." For the most part, I would smile and walk away shaking at my knees. The Spirit of God began visiting me more and more in dreams. Eventually, I began to believe that maybe God had truly called me but I was still afraid.

After much fasting and prayer, in January of 2000 my wife and I met with several members of my family to let them know that I was going into full-time ministry. Most of them laughed and in utter disbelief asked if we had members and who was going to follow me. At the time, I had no followers but only knew that God had called and anointed me to preach the gospel of the Kingdom.

"The Lord is my light and my salvation whom shall I fear ..." (Psalm 27:6)

In July of the same year we launched the ministry. God moved mightily in our services. People started coming from everywhere. My speech impediment disappeared and I spoke clearly, without struggle. *"To God Be The Glory!"*

"YOU CAN DEFEAT FEAR!"

You can defeat the spirit of fear by binding him and casting him out. Fear already knows that whenever you come in alignment with the divine will of God for your life, he has to leave. It has been over ten (10) years since I started preaching and pastoring the church. Although it has not been easy, God has done marvelous things.

PLUNDERING THE SPIRIT OF PRIDE

Believe it or not, the spirit of pride has its share of destructive tactics. Unlike the spirit of fear, pride allows you to go forth with your dreams and will wait until you are successfully working on them and will then seek to destroy you. The Word of God declares that,

"Pride goeth before destruction and a haughty spirit before the fall." (Proverbs 16:18)

I have seen many people eliminated or disqualified from the successful corridors of life because of pride. For some, they were too proud to ask questions or advice and others were simply too proud to give someone else a hand up. People who are overcome by the spirit of pride, for the most part, operate with an independent spirit and seldom feel the need to employ the assistance of others because they think they know everything.

> *"God resisteth the proud, but giveth grace to the humble." (1 Peter 5:6)*

Namaan the Syrian in **2 Kings 5** was the captain of his army but he had leprosy. His handmaid told him about the Prophet Elijah and how God uses him to heal the sick. Namaan was brought to the prophet who instructed him to dip in the Jordan River seven (7) times and God would heal him. Namaan was very angry because he was overtaken by the spirit of pride. After all, he was the captain of the Syrian army and thought that he would have received a much more appealing resolve to his situation.

> *"God takes the foolish things of this world to confound the wise." (1 Corinthians 1:27)*

After much deliberation and convincing, Namaan eventually humbled himself and did as the prophet commanded him. Immediately, his leprosy left and his skin became as smooth as a baby's. If you are going to succeed in life as a believer, you must strive to walk in the spirit of humility. Humility does not mean that you are weak it simply means that you understand that you are who you are, only by the grace of God. It further recognizes that God is the source of your strength, therefore it is easy for you to bless and love some else other than yourself.

> *"Humble yourself there under the mighty hand*
> *of God that He may exalt you in due time:*
> *Casting all your care upon Him; for He cares for*
> *you." (1 Peter 5:7)*

Do not quit! Press your way beyond the stumbling block of pride, a greater blessing awaits you.

DEMOLISHING DOUBT

Doubt is one of the greatest enemies of your faith. The strongman of doubt is fear. If you allow the spirit of doubt to influence you it can cause you to abort your God-given assignment. The spirit of doubt works along with the spirit of abortion and causes you to give up on what God has called you to do. Doubt causes you not to believe what God says.

Whenever the Spirit of God speaks to you and you begin to challenge or question what God is calling you to do then you are being attacked by the spirit of doubt.

Remember, fear comes to intimidate you from even taking a step to move forward. Doubt on the other hand may allow you to move, but in the midst of moving, this sabotaging spirit attacks your mind with disbelief. The spirit of doubt allows you to begin to obey what God is telling you to do and all of a sudden you become uncertain, unsure and even insecure about what you are doing. *Some of the ways the spirit of doubt manifests is through:*

- Indecisiveness/ Hesitation
- Mind Battles
- Unbelief
- Instability
- Discouragement
- Forgetfulness

Doubt will even cause you to reject the wisdom and counsel of God, even when He is trying to get a blessing to you. The spirit of doubt seeks to make you miserable, bitter, frustrated and confused – even in a blessed place. If you do not defeat the spirit of doubt that has been sent to attack you, this demonic spirit can eventually cause you to become bound by the strongman of fear.

Once the stronghold of fear, lodges itself into the mind of an individual the spirit of fear comes in and paralyzes you – preventing you from manifesting all of the promises of God in the fullest measure.

BEWARE OF NEGATIVE
SELF-FULFILLING PROPHECIES

One of the worst forms of doubt is "Self-doubt." It is difficult enough for you to overcome challenges when others do not believe in you. However, one of the greatest battles than any individual must overcome is when he does not believe in himself.

When you succumb to these internal wars then you begin to manifest what are called "negative self-fulfilling prophecies." You begin speaking doubtful words concerning your own life and destiny.

You are with yourself twenty-four hours a day, seven days a week for the rest of your life. If you continue to sow seeds of self-doubt, self-hatred and failure into your own spirit, then you most likely will fail and you have become your own worst enemy. I once heard someone say that if you believe that you can do it you are right, but if you believe that you cannot do it then you are also right. The Word of God clearly states in **Proverbs 23:7**, that *"... as a man thinketh in his heart so is he."*

Self-doubt causes the things that you were once able to do, with no problem, seem almost impossible to you. It causes things to seem to be difficult and somewhat "out-of-reach"; leaving you with feelings of failure and dissatisfaction. You may even attempt something but you do not give it 100% effort or you do not expect it to succeed – all because you doubted yourself.

The spirit of self doubt will cause you to always see others as more capable and qualified while you see yourself as inadequate and limited. If you are going to do anything great for God, you must get rid of the spirit of self-doubt.

DEFEATING THE ENEMY OF DOUBT

As we saw earlier, "whatever you think you are you will eventually become." This is why in **2 Corinthians 10:5**, we are admonished to continually,

"[Cast] down imaginations, and every high thing that exalteth itself against the knowledge of

God, and [bring] into captivity every thought to the obedience of Christ;

In order for you to gain the victory over the spirit of doubt you are going to have to actively and aggressively "pull down" those negative thoughts that perpetually attack your mind. You have to begin to counter them with the Word of God and the promise that God gave you. If God told you that you would be the head and not the tail you have to continue to speak that in your mind.

When thoughts of failure or discouragement come, you cannot allow yourself to meditate on them. You must attack them, pull them down and cause your thoughts to come in agreement with the Word of God. You are a winner. You were destined to win. These are the thoughts that you have to keep in the forefront of your mind until they begin to manifest in your life.

Instead of manifesting negative self-fulfilling prophecies, I say manifest positive ones. Tell yourself what great things you are going to accomplish in life. Every day, set a small goal for yourself, complete it with excellence and celebrate your success. Get in the habit of winning. Do things that you are good at. Begin to build your confidence in what God has blessed you to do.

As the Word of God says in **Romans 12:21**, *"do not be overcome of evil (doubt) but overcome evil (doubt) with good."*

SPIRITUAL PARALYSIS
"If I could only move my right leg..."

Can you imagine being stuck in the same position, unable to move year after year? You watch people come and go but you still find yourself lame and defeated. This is what I call spiritual paralysis.

"The thief cometh not, but for to steal, and to kill, and to destroy: I am come that they might have life, and that they might have it more abundantly." (John 10:10)

Several years ago I took a trip to Ghana, West Africa. I was on a forty day fast and my flight was over twelve hours long. I decided to sleep for the first half of the journey. When I awoke, I felt the need to stretch for a bit. Something strange happened; I could not move my right leg. I was sitting in first class enjoying all of the amenities but when it was time to move, I suddenly realized that I was stuck in my chair. My right leg was numb and had been in one position for so long that it "fell asleep."

Totally embarrassed by my present situation I had to either stay in that semi-paralyzed position or use my other leg and hands to force circulation into it. That is exactly what I did. I started beating and knocking my right leg in an earnest effort to "wake it up!" It was a shocking and painful experience but it worked. After a few minutes, I was able to receive strength and moved my right leg again. It was very easy for me to panic, once I awoke in that situation, but I chose rather to pray and work it out.

If you are going to move forward in life, it is very important that you keep your left and right legs functioning. *"Faith without works is dead, being alone ..."* *(James 2:20)*

"RISE, TAKE UP THY BED AND WALK"

In the gospel of John, chapter five, there was a lame man who had been sitting at the pool of Bethesda for over thirty-eight years. At a certain season, an angel of God came down to trouble the water and whoever stepped in first was healed.

For thirty-eight years he sat there. One day Jesus passed by and asked him why he was still there. He replied that he did not have anyone to put him in. There are times in life when you need to muster enough strength to drag yourself to your deliverance. Jesus had compassion on him and told him to rise, take up his bed and walk. Immediately the man received strength and began walking. Jesus wants you to rise up and walk out of every crippling dilemma you face in life.

A PORTION OF FAITH

According to **Romans 12:3**, God has dealt to each one of us a "measure or portion of faith."

> *"For I say, through the grace given unto me, to every man that is among you, not to think of himself more highly than he ought to think; but to think soberly, according as God hath dealt to every man the measure of faith."*

If you think about it, measurement has to do with size, quantity and portion. A "portion" also deals with capacity, limit or degree. This means that God has blessed each one of us individually with the ability to demonstrate a gift, talent or ability, to a specific degree.

For example, there is a particular member in my church, who decided that she would maintain the cleaning of the church. This was not an appointed position, nor did she ask us if it would be alright to do so. She saw a need and immediately took it as a personal mission to keep the entire church clean and did so, faithfully for years.

In the area of cleaning I observed her as compared to some other persons who also assisted with the cleaning. Once she got to the church she would speak to the secretary or persons there for a brief moment and then begin to sweep.

In thirty minutes, she is finished sweeping without a grain of dirt in the carpet, the bathrooms are sparkling white and she is off to clean and mop the foyer area; the total time is about one hour or an hour and a half the most. Before she left, she inspected the work of others helping her and if it did not meet her standards, she would redo the cleaning, whether sweeping or moping.

In some instances, she would bring other products with her that she happened to find while shopping. Although, cleaning products are in the church's budget, she would ask other persons to help support the purchase of the cleaning products so as to help relieve some of the financial burden off the church. Let me remind you, these were things that I had never asked her to do.

On the other hand persons, given the same assignment sometimes came late or did not show up at all. The areas that they swept had to be swept again. The bathrooms did not have the fresh, clean feeling and they wasted time talking to everybody that came into the building. Furthermore, they constantly complained about how tired they were, after being there for only a short time.

I know that we sometimes talk about the office of the prophet but I truly believe that God has anointed her in the office of "The Cleaner." She has faith to come every day, without being paid, trying to manage personal financial obligations, a family, a business, etc. all because she loves God. Her passion and drive to do whatever it takes to make sure that the Church is kept clean consistently *is a good representation of faith!*

A DEGREE OF FAITH
"Having then gifts differing according to the grace that is given to us, whether prophecy, let us prophesy according to the proportion of faith; ..." (Romans 12:6)

Personally, the Word of God is one of the most practical, "plain-speaking" books that I have ever read. You can literally take every principle in God's Word apply it to your life and see the blessings of God manifest on your behalf. The basic truths of God's word can bring peace, joy and understanding to people's lives. In the book of Romans 12, God shares how each person has a specific function and/or assignment and has been given this by God to function in His Kingdom.

"For as we have many members in one body, and all members have not the same office:"

"So we, being many, are one body in Christ, and every one members one of another."

"Having then gifts differing according to the grace that is given to us, whether prophecy, let us prophesy according to the proportion of faith;"

"Or ministry, let us wait on our ministering: or he that teacheth, on teaching;"

"Or he that exhorteth, on exhortation: he that giveth, let him do it with simplicity; he that ruleth, with diligence; he that sheweth mercy, with cheerfulness."

"Let love be without dissimulation. Abhor that which is evil; cleave to that which is good."
(Romans 12:4 – 9)

This is the thing that I do not understand. If then God is saying to us that I have dealt to every man a measure and a portion of faith then why do we persecute each other because everybody did not give the same amount? Why do we despise another person because they keep singing off tune when you can hit every note?

Why do we think of ourselves as better than someone else because we can remember twenty scriptures and they are struggling to remember **John 3:16?** Why are we so critical and judgmental of each other, when the measure and the portion of faith that you were given was given to you by God?

When you were born, you were born with an assignment. Along with that assignment came the proportion and the measure of faith that you would need to bring your God-given assignment to pass. His ultimate design is that each person's assignment would enhance or compliment the other person's assignment so that the Body of Christ can function. *Remember in Ephesians 4:12, He gave some apostles, prophets, evangelists, pastors and teachers for the purpose of:*
1) Work of the ministry
2) Edifying the body of Christ
3) Perfecting the saints
4) Until Christ be formed in us or better until we all begin to look, act and think like Christ.

The gifts are not for us to try to show others how wonderful or important we are but God has blessed each one of us with a gift so that His church can begin to act and think like the Bride that He desires.

Do you believe that God does not need everybody in the church to be a Prophet? Nor does He need everybody in the church to be in charge. Do you know, God has an established function for each person in the church and it is vitally important that each person functions in his capacity? Each person has been created to function within his portion or measure of faith.

The eye which has been created to see does not have the same function as the ear. The nose which has the capacity to smell does not have the same function as the hand. But each part has a function that is vital and necessary for the effective working of the body. So is it in the Body of Christ- this is why we need each other. It is therefore necessary for each person to abide and fully function in his area or calling.

Many people, in the Body of Christ, waste too much time competing with someone else that is in another lane or category. Even if someone is in the same level of category as you are, do not waste time competing with them. Set your own goals based on the purpose and the divine assignment God has given you.

FAITH THAT DOES NOT WAVER

Now that you understand that faith is simply taking God at His word, let us examine what it means to waver. When I think about wavering, the words that come to mind are: **hesitate,** to be **unsteady,** to **doubt,** to **stagger,** to be **unstable** and lastly, **wave.** I think of the waves in the sea and how they flow back and forth.

In the same way that the tide ebbs and flows, that is the same way that some Christians demonstrate their faith. They believe God today but as soon as something comes to challenge their faith or as soon as it does not look as though the thing will come to pass, they begin to waver – or they begin to doubt.

In the book of **James 1:6,** the Bible states that when you ask God for something, you have to ask in faith – not wavering.

"For he that wavereth is just like the wave of the sea and a double-mind man is unstable in all his ways – Let not that man think he will get anything from God."

STABILIZING YOUR FAITH
*"Before I formed thee in the belly I knew thee;
and before thou camest forth out of the womb I
sanctified thee, and I ordained thee a prophet
unto the nations." (Jeremiah 1:5)*

Some of you know that God has called you. God called some people to be intercessors, evangelists, teachers, and pastors. You know what God has called you to do, but you sit down, waver and allow the spirit of doubt and fear to stop you from fulfilling your God-given assignment here on earth. Some of you were called just like Jeremiah, God said before I formed you in your mother's womb, I knew you, or called you.

God Himself gave Jeremiah a direct word that He had called him to be a prophet to the nations. Jeremiah's first response was, *"Lord, how could that be, I'm only a youth? I cannot speak. God I think you made a mistake."*

He staggered at the word of God. I could hear God saying, *"Jeremiah! Do you know who you are talking to? I am the One who took you from conception and formed you. I am the reason that you are here today. Listen here, son! If it was not for me, you would not be here. So stop talking about what you cannot do, and get busy doing what you can do."*

It's just amazing how we will pray and ask God to use us, and when He answers and gives us an assignment, we say: "Lord, I can't do that!" or "I am too young!" or we say things such as, "Lord, if I do that people will laugh at me."

On the other hand we say, "Lord I want to be rich. I want you to bless me with great riches. I want you to bless my business, and God says, *"Okay! I will do that for you, but I want you to do something for me...*
- ✓ Seek me daily in prayer and the Word
- ✓ Be consistent with your tithe and offering
- ✓ Sow seeds in the kingdom – remembering "it is more blessed to give than to receive"

There are times we approach God with a long list of what we want rather than what we need. At times, He may place a pre-requisite on us and some people begin to falter. There are times that God will challenge you before He releases great things into your hands. This challenge is just a test of obedience and to determine if He could trust us to do whatever He asked if He were to bless us.

Do not hold back when the Spirit of God is calling you to be a blessing. He is not trying to take something *from* you rather; He is trying to get something *to* you.

FAITH AND POWER

Power is simply the ability to perform. It is the release or display of intrinsic strength. The New Testament Greek word *dumanis,* best describes the potency of power which denotes explosive display of one's power or spiritual strength. The other Greek word used is *exousia* which denotes authoritative power which gives you the legal right or might to exercise your will in any situation.

"And lead us not into temptation, but deliver us from evil: For thine is the kingdom, and the power, and the glory, forever. Amen (Matthew 6:13)

Jesus reminded us in Luke 19 that He has given us power over all the powers of the enemy and nothing shall by any means harm us. Do not quit, you have been given power over everything that the enemy tries to bring to you. You have the spiritual strength, ability and kingdom authority to defeat him.

In **Psalm 62:11**, it says, all power belongs unto God. In other words, Satan acts as if he has the power, but God has ALL power. God has transferred the power to mankind. We are the legal authority here on earth, possessing the ability to bind, loose, decree and cast out every demon from hell.

As a child of God and the seed of Abraham, you must rise up at once and begin using your delegated power.

"He giveth power to the faint and to them that have no might he increaseth strength" (Isaiah 40:29)

No matter what you are facing today, God is increasing your strength. My grace is sufficient for thee, for his strength is made perfect in weakness. In fact, when you are weak, that is when God displays His greatest strength. **(2 Corinthians 12:9-10).**

Quitting before exercising your spiritual power means that you have robbed yourself of the opportunity to produce more strength. Further, quitting means that you have not given God the chance to demonstrate His power in your situation.

Wait on the Lord and He shall change and renew your strength and power. You will soon lift your wings and mount up very close to the sun; you shall run and not be weary, walk and not faint neither will you get tired along the way. **(Isaiah 40:31 AMP)**

FAITH AND GLORY

Glory is the grandeur, splendor and excellencies of the brilliance of God revealed. It is the accompanying power and brilliance that manifests the appearance of the presence of God. It is also the tangible evidence that God is present and a witness that His grace and favor is with you. Glory displays the radiance of God but it also includes prestige, power, honor and blessings. Whenever the presence of God's glory shows up, there is an immediate deposit of the anointing which in turn brings automatic prosperity and wealth to your life.

The Hebrew word for glory is *kabod* which means "heavy weight". In other words, God is seeking to make you a heavy weight in the kingdom rather than a light weight. He wants to give you spiritual recognition in the heavy weight category of the kingdom, so that you prosper and conquer every giant along the way.

As you remain steadfast in your faith and commitment to God He will reveal His glory to and through you so, ***Don't Quit!*** The glory is in the finish!
"God is able to do exceeding abundantly above all that you can ask, think or imagine" (Ephesians 3:20)

The three Hebrew boys, in **Daniel 3:1-30**, Shadrach, Meshach and Abednego were faced with the challenge of the fiery furnace of death if they refused* to bow down and worship the golden image erected by King Nebuchadnezzar. They chose not to bow and were hurled into the midst of the furnace, bound hand and feet.

As they were worshipping and praising God, Jesus showed up in the midst of the fire. They were not harmed and the king was so amazed that he commanded everyone to worship the God of Shadrach, Meshach and Abednego. Further because of the supernatural demonstration of God's glory, they were later promoted in the kingdom.

> *16 For which cause we faint not; but though our outward man perish, yet the inward man is renewed day by day.*
>
> *17 For our light affliction, which is but for a moment, worketh for us a far more exceeding and eternal weight of glory;*
>
> *18 While we look not at the things which are seen, but at the things which are not seen: for the things which are seen are temporal; but the things which are not seen are eternal.*
>
> *(2 Corinthians 4:16-18)*

When you do not give up and choose to remain steadfast in the things of God, in due time, He promotes you. For promotion comes not from the east or west but from God.

"For promotion cometh neither from the east, nor from the west, nor from the south."

(Psalm 75:6)

Do not quit, get up and fight for the glory of the Lord awaits you.

CHAPTER 7

THE POWER OF PERSEVERANCE

SURVIVING YOUR DRY SEASON

Have you ever wondered how different people go through the same horrific experience in life; some give up and die never making it out, while others live to tell the story? Those who make it out are the ones I call "*survivors*."

To "*survive*" means that you have not died or given up but rather you have lived through and overcome a devastating ordeal over a difficult period of time. God took the children of Israel out of Egypt and sent them to Canaan, the Promised Land, but they had to cross a wilderness. Because of murmuring and complaining, a journey that should have only taken them fourteen (14) days took them forty (40) years.

Their wilderness was filled with hills and valleys, however, despite their hardships, snakes and insects – God kept them. Their clothes never wore out neither did their shoes grow small. God fed them with manna, sent a cloud by day and a pillar of fire by night and brought forth water out of a rock. He always provided for His people.

"And my God shall supply all of your need according to His riches in glory by Christ Jesus." (Philippians 4:19)

There is an old adage that says, *"Tough times don't last – but tough people do!"* Seasons will come and go but what you do with what you have in each season will determine your final outcome. Everywhere you turn, there is talk about recession. Major corporations have gone *"belly up"*. The stock market has fluctuated. Foreclosures are on the rise. Unemployment is increasing and no matter how much Politicians promise to create jobs, it seems as if they promised in vain.

Regardless of how Economists refer to the economy, whether there is legitimate recession or no recession, the fact remains that people in general, sinner or saint, are having financial challenges. The cost of living is increasing daily. Taxes are on the rise and so are gas prices. Some are wondering if there are truly any real solutions.

I had to seek God for ways to survive. No-one gave me a bag of solutions or a million-dollar check. I had to seek God for my way out. Here are a few of the useful tips He gave my wife and I:

1) First of all acknowledge that you are in debt and or in a bad situation.

2) Create a new mindset

3) Make a decision to change your behavior or come out now by becoming tired of being in that predicament

4) Assess the degree of damage and amount of debt you are in.

5) Be prepared to cut back; crawl until you can walk

6) Do not live above your means, get rid of excess baggage

7) Ask the Holy Spirit to give you wisdom and lead you into a new path of righteousness and prosperity

COMMON "¢ENTS" SOLUTIONS

❖ **Keep a budget**. You must keep a record of your intake and expenses. If your finances are in disorder, your life will also be in disorder. Make a budget and stick to it.

❖ **Carry your lunch to school or work**. You would be amazed at how much money you would save monthly. An average lunch costs about $10. If you purchase lunch five days out of the week, that is $50 weekly, $200 monthly that you are spending.

That money could be used more practically somewhere else.

❖ Do not buy a large amount of groceries_if you never have time to prepare meals at home.

❖ Eat out less. On the other hand, if you do have time, cook and eat more meals at home. This can promote healthy, family time and reduce the amount of money you spend on fast foods and restaurant charges, including tips. *Here's a tip, tip your wife, the next time she cooks for the family!*

❖ Scale back on the cable. Instead of getting deluxe packages, try getting basic cable. Your bill will be reduced drastically. Most times, shows are only repeated anyway, so you are not getting true value for your money.

❖ Car pool. Take turns driving with a friend or neighbor. You will cut your driving time and gas expenses in half.

❖ Do not buy a new car._This one may be a hard pill to swallow, but think about it, a brand new car is considered used and depreciates in value the very second you drive it off the showroom floor. There is nothing wrong with driving a nice used car, until you get to the point where you can maintain that brand new Lexus or Mercedes.

❖ **Check your car or jeep's tire pressure regularly.** Tires that are underinflated and vehicles with dirty air filters can reduce your gas mileage. Ideally, you would want to get more miles for your dollar.

❖ **Wash your own car.** This is a good way to save funds and is a good form of exercise.

❖ **Use cell phones rather than land phones or vice versa.** Whatever plan will save you the most money is the one that you should embrace.

❖ **Purchase clothing that is on sale whenever possible.** This is self explanatory.

❖ **Buy wrinkle free clothing.** You will avoid a huge dry cleaning bill. You may pay a little more initially but in the long run, you will be saving.

❖ **Line dry clothing.** Doing so will help to reduce your energy bill. Furthermore, dryers sometimes can shrink or fade clothing.

❖ **Turn off lights and electronic equipment when not in use.** Again, you will reduce your energy costs. Also the use of energy saving light bulbs will also save money. *Do not run the water when brushing your teeth or when shaving; this also saves you money.*

❖ **Determine how much things you can do on your own.** Going to the experts all of the time can be costly. Learn to sew. Wash and style your hair at home. Watch and read *do it yourself* projects to assist with repairs and improvements around the house. *Spend less money on nonessential items such as DVDs, etc.*

❖ **Cut up excess credit cards.** Use one card for large and necessary purchases. A debit card may be used for everyday or smaller transactions.

❖ **Pay bills immediately!** Pay your credit card bills and loan payments on time. Interest is calculated on the average daily balance of your account for the entire month. So if you pay your bills late, you incur late fees and less money goes to interest and more to the principle.

❖ **Use online banking or the ATMs.** You incur greater fees by engaging the services of a teller inside of the bank. Now, there may be transactions for which you may have to enter the bank. For example, you cannot cash a check at the ATM. Simply, limit these visits to save a few dollars.

❖ **Down-size where necessary_–** For example, you may not need to live in a six-bedroom home if all of your kids are off to school. A small apartment may be more economical, especially if you are paying tuitions.

I conclude with the wisdom of Solomon who said in the book of **Proverbs chapter 7, verse 4:**

> *"Wisdom is the principal thing; therefore get wisdom: and with all thy getting get understanding ... "*

DIG YOUR WAY OUT OR GIVE YOUR WAY OUT!

Fasting , prayer and seeking the face of God are all hallmark "must do's" in order to survive your dry seasons. However, there are vitally important components that I believe truly got my family out of the dangers of debt.

We had already lost so much of our personal possessions including real estate and vehicles but we knew that in order to totally come out of the dry seasons, it was going to take a much greater step of faith. We decided to give away what we had left.

This would mean sowing like we had never sown before. We sowed thousands of dollars into other ministries and into the lives of those who were less fortunate. My wife began clearing out entire closets, giving away everything. We looked foolish but we knew we had to find a way to get God's attention.

But this I say, He which soweth sparingly shall reap also sparingly; and he which soweth bountifully shall reap also bountifully. (2 Corinthians 9:6)

Sowing and reaping is one of the laws of the kingdom but in my opinion it is a principle of life worth holding on to. When you practice giving and sowing this pushes you into a totally different realm from the people who are always just looking for a hand out.

"...it is more blessed to give than to receive."
(Acts 20:35)

I discovered that it is so much easier to follow God when you are a liberal giver. There are no weights and certainly there are no boundaries.

My wife and I started out with what we had. We gave one hundred dollar ($100) seeds, five hundred dollar ($500) seeds. We felt great and soon began to see returns. One day we sowed a one thousand dollar ($1,000) seed and could not believe the results. We stepped out and sowed a five thousand dollar ($5,000) seed. Miracles were happening all around us. I then wondered what would happen if I sowed a ten thousand dollar ($10,000) seed. This was rough, I began rebuking and binding the devil and eventually I got up and sowed it.

As we continued to sow, however, for a short season it seemed as if the seed disappeared in to thin air and was not yielding anything. The enemy began telling me that I should not have sown because it seemed to have gone in reverse. Everything seemed to have gone in reverse. What was I doing wrong, I wondered? The Holy Spirit then showed me that I was looking at my seed for the harvest instead of looking to Jesus, "*The Lord of the Harvest*"

Wow! The ten thousand dollar-seed began producing a supernatural harvest I had never seen before. Supernatural doors were opening and favor began coming from everywhere. I realized then that I tapped into a new dimension of sowing and reaping and I was not about to come out of it any time soon.

"Something Amazing Started Happening"

Everywhere God had us to share our testimony of "Brokenness to Blessedness", people started sowing into our lives. They would call back, screaming about the unexplainable miracles they were receiving. We knew for sure that it was not us but it was obviously a supernatural act of God blessing His people. We learnt a lesson that we would not soon forget- sowing and giving are both contagious and magnetic! It spreads beyond your control and brings back rewards which are unimaginable.

CHAPTER 8

NO IS NOT FINAL!

IT AIN'T OVER!"

When the enemy says, "*No!*", God says , "Yes!" No is absolutely not final. *God is able to do exceeding, abundantly, ABOVE all that you can ask, think or imagine.* When the banks say "No", God says, "... try again, no is not final!" When society says, "No, you cannot achieve this or that", God, says, "I have created you to dominate - go and dominate, my child!" When the doctors say, ".....it is impossible", God says, "...with me, all things are possible!"

I can recall a time in the life of one of my spiritual daughters when she was facing a "NO!" from the doctors. She and her husband were believing God for the miracle of a child. After a couple years of trying to conceive she still did not get pregnant. This was a particularly frustrating time for this couple but they chose to let their faith outweigh fear. She experienced a false positive pregnancy test, endured a series of tests and ultra sounds.

On one occasion, her Gynecologist diagnosed her with an ectopic pregnancy. As we know, if a pregnancy is ectopic, this means that the egg was fertilized outside of the womb, the fetus would not survive. The struggle continued. The no's came repeatedly-but God. God used my wife and I to prophecy over her womb.

Almost immediately, after adding *works* to their faith, this couple conceived. Their delay was not denial. Today they are the parents of two beautiful daughters. A male child was prophesied to this couple as well. "It ain't over until God says it's over"; so I wait to see the manifestation of every godly prophetic word declared over this husband and wife and seal it in the name of Jesus.

There are so many instances in the Word of God where persons had to believe God while facing such distressing challenges such as ***death, debt, disease*** or ***destruction.*** Each one of these persons had a decision to make, either they were going to succumb to their circumstances or they were going to rise up in faith and overcome.

I firmly believe that storms, challenges and difficulties come because God is trying to take us to the next level of faith. He wants you to endure hardness so that the "muscles of your faith" could be strengthened. Once your faith becomes strong there are greater things that you are able to accomplish for God. There are things that you will seek to accomplish that you once thought were impossible.

There are challenges that once threatened you that you will begin to defeat. There are things that made you cry that will not even phase you. You will begin to believe God more. You will begin to trust Him more. You will begin to walk more by faith and not by the limitations of your flesh nor the instability of your emotions.

"NO", IS NOT FINAL IN DEBT!

Have you ever been to the place where you got so discouraged because you ended up in debt? You ended up owing more than you actually had. Creditors are calling! Banks are calling! Some of your possessions have been repossessed and it is only a matter of time before the "Repo Man" comes to take what is left.

Do not lose heart, as I stated earlier, I was right there at one time in my life. It seemed like that season would never end. The enemy did everything he could to make me become fearful, believe that my life was over and that I was a failure. It was not until I took my attention off of my situation and began to seek God for a way out that my life began to change.

I am a living witness that when the enemy says you are not going to ever get out of debt, that this negative decree is not final. Even if you are experiencing a "debt crisis" because of many foolish decisions or careless mistakes that you have made, seek the wisdom of God, He will show you the way out.

SUPERNATURAL DEBT CANCELLATION

Consider the account of the widow woman who came to the prophet Elisha, plagued by creditors and limited in resources. They were not only going to take her possessions but her two sons were going to become bond slaves in order to pay off the debt that her husband had left behind.

Hopeless and destitute, she turns to the prophet to seek counsel on how to preserve her household and save her sons.

[1]Now there cried a certain woman of the wives of the sons of the prophets unto Elisha, saying, Thy servant my husband is dead; and thou knowest that thy

servant did fear the LORD: and the creditor is come
to take unto him my two sons to be bondmen.
²And Elisha said unto her, What shall I do for thee?
tell me, what hast thou in the house? And she said,
Thine handmaid hath not anything in the house, save
a pot of oil.
³Then he said, Go, borrow thee vessels abroad of all
thy neighbors, even empty vessels; borrow not a few.
⁴And when thou art come in, thou shalt shut the door
upon thee and upon thy sons, and shalt pour out into
all those vessels, and thou shalt set aside that which is
full.
⁵So she went from him, and shut the door upon her
and upon her sons, who brought the vessels to her;
and she poured out.
⁶And it came to pass, when the vessels were full, that
she said unto her son, Bring me yet a vessel. And he
said unto her, There is not a vessel more. And the oil
stayed.
⁷Then she came and told the man of God. And he said,
Go, sell the oil, and pay thy debt, and live thou and
thy children of the rest.
(2 Kingdom 4:1 – 7)

Her obedience to the man of God, turned her entire
situation around. Her "debt crisis" became the catalyst

by which she had become blessed beyond measure. "No!" is not final – not even in debt!

"NO", IS NOT FINAL IN DEATH!

At some point in all of our lives we have experienced a loss, whether it was the loss of a family member or friend, the loss of a beloved pet or even the loss of a job. Even biologically, some of the cells in the human body die daily. Death is considered to be the end of or ceasing of a thing. The Bible declares that death is not a respecter of persons. It visits you at every stage and every level. However, death does not have to be final. There is still hope even in death.

Consider the account of Jairus' daughter in the book of Luke chapter 8. Jarius was a ruler in the synagogue and a very prominent man in his community. When his daughter died her family wept uncontrollably. Jesus had just performed several miracles prior and was about to undertake another. When he got to the ruler of the Synagogue's house, he announced to the crowd that she was only sleeping. Doubt filled the room and so He dispersed all of the mourners and only took three of his disciples with Him to her bed side. Taking her by the hand, He called her back to life. Jesus is the resurrection and the life. *"No"*, is not final even in death.

"NO", IS NOT FINAL IN DISEASE!

There are numerous accounts in the Bible where Jesus demonstrated His power over sickness and disease and commanded total healing. It is not the will of God that you should be plagued by sickness and disease but it is the will of God that you prosper and be in health even as your soul prospers **(3 John 2)**. God not only wants to heal you but He wants to make you whole.

Whenever you are faced with a sickness or disease, do not claim it as your own. Send it back to the pit of hell from whence it came and continue to declare that by the stripes of Jesus you are healed.

⁵But he was wounded for our transgressions, he was bruised for our iniquities: the chastisement of our peace was upon him; and with his stripes we are healed (Isaiah 53:5)

Sickness and disease can be introduced by way of generational curses. You do not have to accept this. Do not accept a death sentence. Do not accept the "No"- no you cannot recover, no you cannot be healed....No! Do not accept these negative decrees from the enemy. Pray to God, the Father breaking every generational curse and repenting of the sins of your ancestors.

"....visiting the iniquity of the fathers upon the children, and upon the children's children, unto the third and to the fourth generation." (Isaiah 34:7)

God will hear and honor your prayer of faith. You do not have to accept any report of sickness or disease in your life *"No"*, is not final even in disease!"

"NO", IS NOT FINAL WHEN FACING DANGER & DESTRUCTION!

There are times in life that you might have experienced some sort of danger. Your very life could have been in jeopardy. I can recall an incident where one of my members faced danger and destruction. She was in a store and a robbery was taking place. A gun was pointed directly in her face.

The angel of the LORD encampeth round about them that fear him, and delivereth them (Psalm 34:7)

She came out of that ordeal unharmed. The Lord said "No!" to the impending danger and delivered her from destruction.

When you live in, abide and dwell in the presence of the Lord, He delivers you from destruction and the plans of your enemy to take you out.

[1]He that dwelleth in the secret place of the most High shall abide under the shadow of the Almighty

5Thou shalt not be afraid for the terror by night; nor for the arrow that flieth by day;

[6]Nor for the pestilence that walketh in darkness; nor for the destruction that wasteth at noonday.

[7]A thousand shall fall at thy side, and ten thousand at thy right hand; but it shall not come nigh thee. (Psalm 91:1, 5 - 7)

Be encouraged, my friend. Remember that whenever you receive an adverse report, whenever you are *told* "No!", turn that no around and tell the devil, it is "On!" You will not quit, but will stay in the fight ".

CHAPTER 9

DON'T QUIT – TRY AGAIN!

NO RETREAT! NO SURRENDER!

As a pastor, there have been countless occasions that I have had to counsel my members and persons from the community who were on the verge of giving up. The stresses of life were weighing them down. They were ready to wave the white flag of surrender. Others were ready to throw in the towel and quit.

I can recall one of my members who was greatly challenged, financially. She had so many deductions coming from her salary that by the end of the day, her gross pay was mere cents. She was barely able to afford to pay her tithes. However, I encouraged her to remain faithful and honor God with her tithes. She would tell you that unscrupulous thoughts sometimes challenged her. She was tempted to play the lottery or *buy numbers*. This is only a game of chance and does not profit an individual.

She continued to trust God. She did not give up during the challenging times that her vehicle remained park because there was no gas in it or during the times she and her husband had no vehicle at all. She trusted God when the only thing her family had to eat sometimes was mere crackers and a cup of tea. She trusted God to provide for her family and meet her needs.

As time passed, she continued to work hard on her job. Eventually she was promoted and her finances turned around. She did not quit even when times were difficult. Today, she can travel, resides comfortably in her own home and just recently bought a jeep. God is faithful. You must trust Him to take care of you. Even David said:

"I have been young, and now am old; yet have I not seen the righteous forsaken, nor his seed begging bread" (Psalm 37:25)

The testimonies are so great and I thank God for His faithfulness. Another praise report comes to mind. There is a couple in my ministry who were experiencing marital problems. They were separated, living apart because of the wife's involvement in an extra marital affair. The husband was determined to fight for this marriage even when his wife did not want to have anything to do with him, the ministry or God. He refused to quit. Sometimes he would come to counseling by himself. He attended services regularly, prayed, fasted and sowed seeds.

The prayers of the righteous availed much! Because this brother was so determined to fight for his marriage, God heard and answered his prayers. Today, this couple is reunited, living happily together raising their daughter. They are active members of the local congregation and a testimony that God can heal, restore and mend marriages.

If you are experiencing marital challenges right now, do not quit, do not give up, and do not walk out. If you are willing to allow Him to, God can and will save your marriage.

PERSEVERANCE PAYS

Perseverance positions you to stick, stay and hold on. It is steadfastness in accomplishing your God given task despite delay or difficulty. The biblical account of Noah is a great example of perseverance. In total obedience to God, Noah spent 120 years building an ark, when he had no idea of what rain was. He did not quit building even when others mocked him. He was focused and conscious to the assignment that God had given him.

"And God said unto Noah.... [14] Make thee an ark of gopher wood..... [17] And, behold, I, even I, do bring a flood of waters upon the earth, to destroy all flesh....and everything that is in the earth shall

die... ²² Thus did Noah; according to all that God commanded him, so did he." (Genesis 6)

TENACITY KEEPS YOU ON THE WALL

"When the going gets tough and the tough gets going – tenacity is what keeps you stuck to your assignment"

In addition, Nehemiah can be identified as one whose persistence and tenacity, was the driving impetus that enabled him to stay in the fight and not quit. Nehemiah was the King's cupbearer and was greatly distressed over the fact that his home, the sacred city, Jerusalem lay vulnerable because the walls were broken down and its gates were burned with fire.

Gates represents access, entrance and exit. They also represent protection. If a city's gate was in a state of disrepair, that city was susceptible to being attacked and overtaken by its enemies. This caused Nehemiah to be extremely burdened.

.... the wall of Jerusalem also is broken down, and the gates thereof are burned with fire.

*⁴And it came to pass, when I heard these words,
that I sat down and wept, fasted, and prayed
before the God of heaven.....
(Nehemiah 1:3-4)*

King Artaxerxes granted Nehemiah permission and extended favor for the rebuilding of the wall *(Nehemiah 2:1-5)*. This was a big task for Nehemiah especially knowing that he did not have any money. He started the rebuilding process but was constantly inundated with attacks from the enemy; in an effort to stop the work and force him to come down from building the wall.

*¹⁹ "But when Sanballat the Horonite, and Tobiah the
servant, the Ammonite, and Geshem the Arabian,
heard it, they laughed us to scorn...." (Nehemiah 1)*

Whenever God has spoken a word over your life regarding your divine assignment, the enemy comes in and seeks to discourage you out of position. Satan will hire people to slander, scorn and even laugh at what God has called you to do. He uses arrows of false accusation, persecution, despair, sickness, fear and doubt to demobilize you. Those closest to you may even forsake and abandon you. However, you must not quit! You must not give up on your God-given assignment. Gird yourself with the full armor of God and stay on the wall!

THE MIRACLE OF THE BUILDING

God will give you kingdom tenacity, to stay on your assignment, just as He gave Nehemiah. When we started the ministry, in a beautiful storefront building, we eventually outgrew it and decided to move. God then took us from the store front building into our own property. We immediately began having breakthrough Revival services under what we called "The white glory tent." The presence of God would come and people were being delivered and set free in almost every service.

During the Revivals, the move of God was so powerful; but during the rainy season when the storms came, we would get wet and soaked. I began prophesying and telling people that God was going to send us a building, debt-free. We did not have much money at the time but we had faith. Eventually, we ordered a building out of Arkansas, USA with no idea how we were going to pay for it. We kept praying until one day we got a call from a friend who said she had a blessing for us.

When I got to her office, she gave me a check for the exact amount we needed to ship and purchase the frame for the building. Everything began falling into place as God raised up young men within the ministry with skills to help with the building process.

These were young men who came off of drugs and out of gangs with very little, yet the Spirit of God equipped them and with gladness they labored with me to do the work. The enemy fought us each step of the way. Many people including pastors laughed at us. There were days that I felt like giving up, but I could not. Something kept me going. We were building a huge building debt-free without borrowing any monies from the bank. That alone made the devil angry.

Every time we got to another phase, people came to the office and sowed. God was sending us miracle money without us having to go to the bank to get a loan. To date we are almost completed constructing our miracle building – the people are not laughing anymore! *To God Be The Glory!*

CHAPTER 10

BACK IN THE FIGHT!

RESTORATION HAS COME

God is the God of total restoration. Everything shall be restored. This is so amazing! The kingdom of God is the only entity that guarantees a one hundred percent (100%) return on your investment. As the Word of God says in **Joel 2:25**,

> *"I will restore the years that the locust have eaten, the cankerworm and the caterpillar, my great army that I sent among you."*

In other words, whatever has been stolen, taken or lost from your life, God is going to give it back to you. It is your mandate to keep your faith strong, believing God that your "payday" is at hand.

> *"...Weeping may endure for a night but joy cometh in the morning..." (Psalm 30:5)*

For years, we, as believers have been told that once you give your life to Jesus everything will be alright. This common belief led many to believe that the life that God intends for us to live will be a life of ease and comfort. But if we truly give our lives to Jesus and set Him as the example that we will follow we will see that His life was one that encountered many great challenges.

We see Him facing adversaries, false accusers, religious leaders, fierce critics and even death as He sought to do the will of the Father. On the other hand, the sacrifice that He suffered was worth the joy that He experiences every time a soul is saved or someone calls on His name and they are set free. All of this came at a great price to him but one that He was willing to pay. *(Hebrews 12:2)*

God is truly a restorer and I see things now from my vantage point. He has blessed my life tremendously. Everything that I lost has been restored and He continues to bless me daily because I believe in Him.

"He restoreth my soul, he leadeth me in the paths of righteousness for his name sake...."
(Psalm 23:3)

RECOVER ALL – A TIME TO PURSUE
"Thou shalt surely pursue, overtake, overthrow them and without fail recover all...." (1 Samuel 30)

Sometimes right while we are in the midst of the battle field, the enemy comes in to steal our blessings. The bible tells us here that David was in Ziklag doing what God called him to do. While doing so, the

Amalekites sneaked in his camp and stole all of their wives, children and possessions.

David became so distressed that he sought God for a combat plan. God told him to pursue and overtake his enemies. You must seek God for your combat plan. Total recovery is His will concerning you. David got back everything they took and more.

YOUR WEALTHY PLACE

I thank God for the anointing and grace He has given me to persevere. The things I could not understand in my early days, I certainly understand now. You see, God was in it all along. God is the One who causes you to take the pathway you are on. He is not surprised by your many bumps, curves, pot holes and roadside dilemmas. His ultimate quest is to bring you to Himself and usher you into a wealthy place.

> *[10] For thou, O God, hast proved us: thou hast tried us, as silver is tried.*

> *[11] Thou broughtest us into the net; thou laidst affliction upon our loins.*

> *[12] Thou hast caused men to ride over our heads; we went through fire and through water: but*

> *thou broughtest us out into a wealthy place.*
> *(Psalm 66:10-12)*

ANOINTED TO PROSPER

To be "anointed" means to be smeared on by the Spirit of God to do or accomplish or carry out a specific function. It is the notable ability to live as God ordained you to – prospering in every area. In the old days, most Christians believed that God wanted His children to be poor. This is totally contrary to the will and word of God. He said, "it is not His will that anyone should perish ..."

Further, in **3 John 1:2**, it says, *"Beloved I wish above all things that thou mayest prosper ..."*

Prosperity means that you are living a whole and complete life, where nothing is missing or lacking. God wants His children to live a life of complete wholeness. If you find yourself living a life of hardship and poverty, make a decision today to make a total change. Prosperity has already been available to you by the Spirit of God; it is your choice to embrace it.

Paul said everything that he had gained; he counted them as dung for the gospel's sake. I have also gained a lot in my lifetime. I also lost a lot, but today, God has brought me to a wealthy place and He will bring you there too. Begin today by trusting (totally relying and depending on God.)

> *¹They that trust in the LORD shall be as mount Zion, which cannot be removed, but abideth for ever.*
>
> *²As the mountains are round about Jerusalem, so the LORD is round about his people from henceforth even forever.*
>
> *³For the rod of the wicked shall not rest upon the lot of the righteous; lest the righteous put forth their hands unto iniquity (Psalm 125:1-3)*

God brings His children to a place where He increases you and blesses you to be a blessing. It is a kingdom principle that the more you give, you position yourself to receive that much more.

> *"Give and it shall be given unto you; good measure, pressed down shaken together and running over shall men pour into your bosom."*

SLAYING YOUR GIANTS

Now that your strength has been renewed you have been anointed to walk in kingdom power. You are a giant slayer, just like David. You will not fall in the face of your giants. *Five smooth stones of faith, power, praise, might and glory* is what brought Goliath down. God is now giving you the same opportunity to bring yours down.

God has equipped you in this season to not only slay your giants, but to take their heads off. When David killed Goliath, he took his head off to remind Israel and their enemies that they had the power to crush the head of their adversaries. It also denotes that the Nation of Israel will crush the heads of their enemies. And, as we are spiritual Israel, we have the same power and ability to do the same. This is a sign to each believer that you also have power to crush the head of every giant in your life.

Through the Blood of Jesus Christ, God will give you the necks of your enemies. No more will they laugh and scorn you, but God will cause them to bow and honor you.

"The abundance of the seas shall be converted unto you. The wealth and treasures of the nations shall

come unto you. The sons of strangers shall build up thy walls and their kings shall minister unto you; your gates will never close again but shall be opened continually so that wealthy people will bring their riches and possessions to you." (Isaiah 60:5 – 11)

YOUR REWARD IS IN THE FINISH

Jesus came to make walking by faith possible, not easy but to those who are able to endure through every level and testing of their faith the joy of the reward will be worth it!

"Therefore my beloved brethren, be steadfast, immoveable, always abounding in the work of the Lord, knowing that your labor is not in vain in the Lord." (1 Corinthians 15:58)

To be steadfast means not wavering, not changing but being firm. Further, the word immoveable means: not changing in one's purpose, not moved emotionally or spiritually. And finally, to abound is to continue thriving in the things of the Lord.

Why does God want you to be steadfast, immoveable, always abounding in the work of the Lord? Because God knows that it will be worth it in the end.

He knows that there is a reward for serving Him and in the end; your faith will bring a reward in your life and in the life of many others. So don't quit! You have got to finish, for the glory and the reward are in the "finish!"

I want to remind you again, DON'T QUIT! GET BACK IN THE FIGHT! Maintain your peace, joy, faith and anointing in the Lord!

INDEX

MEET APOSTLE DR. EDISON NOTTAGE

Apostle Edison Nottage, as he is affectionately called, is a man of Vision, Faith & Power. He accepted Jesus at the age of sixteen and immediately began witnessing by sharing the gospel of the kingdom with others. He became an active and faithful member at his local church, where he served as a youth minister and aid to his pastor. Apostle Nottage is married to Prophetess Mattie Nottage and they have four beautiful children.

After much prayer and fasting Apostle Edison and his wife answered the call of God to full-time Ministry. God had spoken clearly to them instructing them to go forth into ministry raising the standard of righteousness and holiness in the lives of young people and families.

In July, 2000 Apostle Edison Nottage, along with his, wife founded and established *Believers Faith Outreach Ministries, International* in beautiful Nassau, Bahamas. They are esteemed as dynamic, anointed tag-team partners, called to the kingdom for such a time as this.

The mission of Believers Faith Outreach Ministries International is to break through the barriers of tradition and develop a righteous army of believers who will revolutionize the Islands of the Caribbean, the United States of America and the world.

Apostle Nottage is a powerful teacher of the word. His practical teachings on faith and prosperity, and the demonstration of the power of God has changed the lives of many people in our nation and around the world. He has conducted many breakthrough revivals, conferences, and seminars on parks, school campuses, and convention centers. Apostle Nottage is also a successful entrepreneur.

He and his wife have founded several organizations which are presently transforming lives around the world. Some of which are: The Mending The Marriage Ministry, the "When Lions Roar" Men's Ministry, the Youth In Action Group, Boys II Men Club, Girls of Excellence Club, Youth Back To The Cross Ministry, and The Global Dominion Network.

In addition, Apostle Nottage has been actively involved in youth and family ministry for over twenty years. Dr. Nottage's aim is to equip believers to take authority in every area of their lives, gaining victory over the enemy of their soul and to build up the kingdom of God.

*Please contact our office to request a complete listing of CD and DVD titles.

For more information on bookings or to place an order for products, please contact:
Believers Faith Outreach Ministries, International
P.O. Box SB-52524
Nassau, Bahamas
www.believersfaith.com
Tel/Fax: (954) 237-8196 or (242) 698-1383

Believers Faith Breakthrough Ministries,
International
6511 Nova Dr.
Suite #193
Davie, Florida, 33317
www.mattienottage.org

Tel/Fax: (888) 825-7568

Made in the USA
Columbia, SC
16 March 2019